Passenger Ships Italian Style

By
William H. Miller

[signature] May 1997

Published, 1996, by
Carmania Press

Unit 224, Station House, 49 Greenwich High Road,
London SE10 8JL
Book production by Roger Hardingham
Printed by The Amadeus Press, Huddersfield, West Yorkshire
© William H. Miller and Carmania Press
ISBN 0 9518656 4 1

Contents

Acknowledgements

A great many people have been extraordinarily generous in helping me write this book, in sharing anecdotes, photographs and prized collectibles and papers. I am especially grateful to Anthony Cooke and his fine Carmania Press for accepting the project. It was inspired by my visits to Genoa and other Italian ports and by various trips on Italian and former Italian passenger ships - among them the *Raffaello, Cristoforo Colombo, Meridian* (ex-*Galileo Galilei*), *Ocean Islander* (ex-*San Giorgio*), *Sea Breeze* (ex *Federico C.*), *Eugenio C., Carla C., Fairstar, Fairsea, Ausonia, Achille Lauro, Queen Frederica* (ex-*Atlantic*), *Homeric, Oceanic, Romanza* (ex-*Aurelia*), and two of the more contemporary generation, the *Crown Princess* and *Renaissance III*.

Maurizio Eliseo, the author of that splendid book on the glorious *Rex*, has been prominent in reading through and checking the manuscript and in offering very useful additional information and notes. His help has been invaluable. I would also like to thank Frank Braynard, Tom Cassidy, Frank and Joan Duffy, Dick Faber, Bill Fox, Andy Hernandez, Eric Johnson, Arnold Kludas, Jan Loeff, Neil McGuinness, Mitchell Mart, Vincent Messina, A. Molinari, Bert Novelli, Bob Pelletier, Victor Rollo, Sal Scannella, Willie Tinnemeyer, Gregory Vossos and Joe Wilhelm. Special thanks to Stephen Card for his superb cover.

As always, those great maritime photographers and collectors have been an exceptional help. They include J.K. Byass, Michael Cassar, Luis Miguel Correia, Alex Duncan, Michael D. J. Lennon, Ove Neilsen, Paolo Piccione, Schiffsfotos Jansen, Antonio Scrimali, the late Victor Scrivens, Roger Sherlock, Everett Viez, Steffen Weirauch and Vic Young and Len Sawyer.

Bringing these great ships to further life, anecdotes and other insightful recollections have been provided by Captain Elvio Arimondo, Scott Baty, Captain Adriano Borreani, Dr. David Bright, Captain Lorenzo Calvillo, Captain Claudio Ciappina, Len Chapman, Captain Dimitrios Chilas, Captain Antonio Da Rosa, Captain Franco Donnino, Captain Narciso Fossati, Ugo Frangini, George Greishaber, Vito Matti, Professor Dr. William McLean, Captain Renato Piovino, Captain D. Julian Rapier, Rino Rivieccio, Giancarlo Roccatagliata and Captain Mario Vespa.

Existing companies and organizations that have assisted include the Costa Line, Holland America Line, Moran Towing & Transportation Company, Norshipco, the P&O Group, the Port Authority of New York & New Jersey, Princess Cruises, the South China Morning Post and the World Ship Society. Other help came from firms which, alas, are no more: the Argentine State Line, Flying Camera Inc., the Incres Line and Ocean Cruise Lines.

And last, but by no means least, very warmest thanks to my family and to Abe Michaelson.

Foreword

by Sal Scannella

I accepted with great pleasure the invitation from Bill Miller to write a few words to present this new book on Italian Passenger Ships. Ever since I was a youngster and sailed from New York to Naples on the SS *Independence*, I have been in love with ocean liners. I jumped at the opportunity to work for the Italian Line in 1965 at their main office then located in "Steamship Row" in downtown Manhattan. This just happened to be the year of the maiden arrival of both the *Michelangelo* and the *Raffaello*, Italian Line's new prides and joys. What a festive time this was for the Italian Line and for me!

I began at 19 years of age as a clerk and booking agent in Tourist Class and worked my way up to Assistant Advertising and Promotion Manager. What fun I had producing brochures (that I used to collect as a child), taking Coast Guard cutters out to board the inbound liners to take photos for use in ads, and helping arrange embarkation for the likes of the Duchess of Windsor, Alfred Hitchcock, Ed Sullivan and many others that loved the splendid Italian Line service and cuisine. We were about 90 employees at the New York office, mostly of Italian and Italian-American descent. It was like a big family and till this day we have a reunion party every couple of years. Fortunately, I was able to salvage a good deal of Italian Line memorabilia prior to the closing of the office (in 1976) when all else was thrown away.

Nothing in my life could have been more exciting than my years with the Italian Line. It was like being paid to partake in your favorite hobby every day. Italian Line was also the US general agent for Lloyd Triestino, which operated the Italy-Australia service. We also represented the other companies in the Finmare Group, namely the Adriatica and Tirrenia Lines.

I am so happy that Bill has decided to write a book on Italian liners. I could think of no finer writer to do it, especially since I know that the Italian Line was dear to his heart as well.

'Luxury Liner Row' - the Italian Line passenger ships were often included in those great gatherings of ocean liners along New York City's West Side piers in the 1950s and '60s. In this view from July 1962, the *Vulcania* is at the forefront of this collection. Beyond is the little Turkish passenger ship *Giresun* (on a special voyage from Istanbul), then the French Line's *Flandre* and the new *France*, Cunard's *Queen Elizabeth* and then the National Hellenic American Line's *Queen Frederica* and Hamburg-Atlantic Line's *Hanseatic*.

Richard C. Faber collection

Introduction

Genoa is Italy's biggest and busiest port. There are cruiseships and drydocks, grain elevators and melancholically deserted warehouses (indeed, the age of efficient containerization has long since taken hold). Lovely hills surround, almost caress, the port and an outer breakwater completes the enclosure. Not far away are resorts like Portofino and Rapallo, the big shipbuilding yards at Sestri (where the likes of the mighty old *Rex*, the immortal *Andrea Doria* and the giant *Michelangelo* where born) and then, in a sort of reverse process, the scrapyards at La Spezia (the great French *Liberte* and the magnificent *Leonardo Da Vinci* were among those finished-off there). Genoa, once the hub of a vast international passenger ship network - with sailings to and from places like Boston and Buenos Aires and Brisbane - shows all the signs of transition : added container cranes, a hefty new floating drydock for supertankers and giant bulkers, and - then firmly in the design stage - a rehabilitated passenger-cruise terminal. The year of my visit was 1989, and it helped to inspire this book, a work just about the many Italian, near-Italian and Italian-built passenger ships. As I stood along the passenger quay, I could almost see the *Cristoforo Colombo* sailing to New York and the *Anna C.* for South America and the *Galileo Galilei* for Australia.

The Stazione Marittima has a majestic, ornate Rococo facade. Built pre-war, in the Mussolini era, it was once the terminal for big Atlantic liners. But by 1989, it had become rather faded glory: dim lighting, empty shops, peeling paint. It was long overdue for a complete refacing - the interiors (especially for weary travellers just in from long connecting, international flights) were downright depressing and certainly a steambath on humid summer afternoons. During my weekend visit, in early July, over 2,000 passengers were to set sail on three cruiseships - two Italians, the *Ausonia* and the *Eugenio Costa*, and the Greek *Odysseus*. On the following day, a Sunday, another 1,500 would depart aboard the *Enrico Costa* and the Soviet *Shota Rustavelli.* Also, at least a half-dozen Tirrenia Line ferries leave each day, heavily loaded with passengers, cars and trucks bound for holiday spots in Corsica and Sardinia. Tucked away at the time and quite lifeless-looking, the onetime Swedish *Stockholm* (dating from 1948 and the ship which collided with the Genoa-based *Andrea Doria* eight years later) was at a backwater berth. Despite her then 42 years and the supposed "exhaustion" of her original diesels, she was apparently to be rebuilt for Starlauro Cruises as the cruiseship *Positano* (*Sorrento* had been the intented name just a few weeks before). She had come from Oslo, where she had last been serving as an accommodation ship for Asian refugees.

The container-cargo berths seemed busy enough: a lofty Japanese NYK Line ship kept those goose-like dockside cranes busy and then quietly slipped off to make way for a Taiwanese Evergreen Line ship, similarly in the over-50,000-ton class. The vast, local Fincantieri shipyards were evidently facing a dilemma now well known to similar facilities: a lack of work. All of the big drydocks were empty, the cranes were in rather orderly, but idle formation and the three Lloyd Triestino containerships at berth appeared to be laid-up and out-of-work. An enormously muscular crane ship was lying at an outer berth, seemingly not under repair but merely awaiting a call to duty. At an adjacent, far less visible slip, there was one novelty: the bare steel hulk of a former Swedish containership was being made over as the cruiseship *Costa Marina*. She would be due in about a year, for Genoa-based sailings.

By late afternoon, a gentler, more yellowed haze hung over the Port of Genoa. The *Ausonia,* then the *Eugenio Costa* and finally the *Odysseus* sailed off - as did all those Tirrenia ferries. A quiet mood, interrupted only by the sounds of crying seabirds, took hold. Italy's busiest seaport seemed to have gone to sleep.

It has been a great and thorough pleasure to compile this book. Hopefully, it will revive some memories of Passenger Ships Italian Style.

William H. Miller
Secaucus, New Jersey, USA
Autumn 1995

for
VINCENT MESSINA
friend, ship historian, world traveller

Chapter One

Italian Line

The Dowagers

"The *Saturnia* and the *Vulcania* were very strong ships, always superb at sea. After the Second World War, they carried tens of thousands of immigrants to America. Some immigrant babies were born on board and then often called *Saturnia* or *Vulcania* as a middle name. They were immensely popular and immensely profitable", so recalled Captain Narciso Fossati, a junior officer in these near-sisterships in the early 1950s. Then, in that first post-war decade, much of Europe was still deep in recovery from the ravages of the 1939-45 War. Italy was far from an exception. These two ships were not only the most important, but also the largest ships in the Italian merchant fleet. They were some 24,000 tons each.

Italy's glorious pre-war liners were gone, mostly bombed, set afire, sabotaged and then given over to salvage and scrapping crews. In the late 1940s, the nation's sole Blue Riband champion, the 51,000-ton *Rex*, lay on her side, capsized in an Allied air attack in September 1944. Wreckers worked slowly on her burnt-out hulk. The equally splendid *Conte Di Savoia*, a 48,500-tonner, had also sunk. Briefly, in 1945, in a burst of optimism,there was some thought to restoring what had been one of the 1930s' most beautiful liners, but only as an all-third class, emigrant ship for the South American trade. But in the final appraisal,it would have been impractical - both materials and money were in short supply. Others like the pre-war *Augustus* and *Roma*, and the *Giulio Cesare* and *Duilio* were gone as well. Two sisters, the 1932-built *Neptunia* and *Oceania*, were actually sunk on the very same day, on September 18th 1941. In the end, by 1945-46, only four large Italian liners remained: the aforementioned *Saturnia* and *Vulcania,* and another pair of near-sisters, the *Conte Biancamano* and the *Conte Grande.* They had been in American hands during the War and then, quite thoughtfully, were returned to an otherwise denuded Italian Line. The Genoa head office turned its full

Returned to Italy by the US Government just after the Second World War, the *Vulcania* (left) and the *Saturnia* reopened the Italian Line's Naples-Genoa-New York express run in 1947. In a very rare occasion, they are seen together at Genoa. *Jan Loeff collection*

Above and left: Two of Italy's most successful, most popular and most enduring passenger liners. The *Vulcania (above)* is docked at Palermo.   *EverettViez collection*
The *Saturnia (left)* - with the distinguishing upsweep in her funnel - is shown sailing from Naples.   *Eric Johnson*

attention to the restoration of these ships. The *Saturnia* and *Vulcania* would be refitted to much of their pre-war style and even splendor; the *Conte Biancamano* and *Conte Grande* would be modernized considerably, mostly because of the enormous alterations made by the US Government, who had used them as busy and valiant troop transports.

Post-war Italy was quite desperate. The economy was shattered and now heavily dependant on American aid. Its people, weary from war, now feared the future. There were Communist threats and even clouds of, perhaps, World War III. Many were jobless, even homeless. And so, an enormous exodus began - the Italians themselves, refugees, displaced persons, Eastern Europeans who were flowing over the Italian borders. Emigration lines had to be re-established and with great urgency. And, of course, regular passenger ship links with appropriate first and cabin class quarters were needed as well - less for tourists than for

the political and business clientele, the merchants, the post-war military officialdom, the recovery teams and, as always on Italian passenger ships, those entourages to and from the Vatican. The Italian links to the outside world had to be restored.

The Italian Line, governed by those first post-war ministries of marine in Rome, prepared to re-instate its two most important pre-war trades - the "North Atlantic express run" between Naples, Genoa and New York, and also the largely emigrant route to the East Coast of South America, to Brazil, Uruguay and Argentina. Themselves damaged in the War, shipyards at Genoa, at Naples and at Monfalcone (near Trieste) turned their attention to restoring these four liners.

The *Saturnia* and *Vulcania* had been built in the mid 1920s, in an age when motorships were the new moderne. Italy's passenger ship owners were then quite separate and these two were ordered as the new flagships of the Trieste-based Cosulich Line. Cosulich's interests were in the Adriatic trades, sailing out of Trieste as well as Venice. The new ships would go on the premium New York route. In those boom years of vital liner services, especially on the Atlantic, they carried no less than four classes of passengers. The 23,900-ton *Saturnia* could carry, for example, a total of 2,197 passengers - 279 in luxurious first class, 257 in less ornate second class, 309 in very moderate third class and finally 1,352 in austere, mostly dormitory-style fourth class. The *Saturnia* came first, in September

1927, with special introductory sailings from Trieste and Venice to Rio de Janeiro, Santos, Montevideo and Buenos Aires. She started her New York sailings in the following February. The *Vulcania*, which at first was to have been called *Urania*, joined her on the North Atlantic in December 1928. Technically, with their powerful Burmeister & Wain diesels, they were among the fastest (top speed 19 knots) and the largest motorliners of the day.

In 1932, under the personal edict of Mussolini, all of Italy's major passenger lines were consolidated. They would be controlled by Finmare, which was based in Rome. Increasing foreign-flag competition plus the effects of the worldwide Depression prompted all of this. Three companies, which ran services to North and South America, including Cosulich, were merged and restyled as the Italian Line, "Italia" to most Europeans and to the Italians themselves. And so, while they remained in their original service from the Adriatic, the *Saturnia* and *Vulcania* joined a newly created fleet, one eventually headed by the brand new *Rex* and *Conte Di Savoia*. Actually, the final integration of the *Saturnia* and *Vulcania* was completed five years later, in 1937. Now, they were officially and completely part of the Italian Line. Just before, in 1935, both had been given costly refits. They were re-engined with more powerful, Italian-built Fiat diesels. They could now muster an additional 2 knots when needed, up to a full 21 knots. They were also used briefly by the Mussolini government for troop voyages out to East Africa for the Abyssinian campaign.

"The *Saturnia* and *Vulcania* were among the most beautiful liners ever built. Their first class public rooms especially were like travelling in a royal castle," according to Professor Dr. William McLean, who made over a dozen crossings in the pair. "Unlike all other liners, the positions of captain and other high officers were always held by members of the Cosulich family, the ships' original owners. I especially remember Captain Aristide Cosulich."

"The ballroom was tropical in nature," noted Dr McLean, "and was famed for its great glass dome and double row of gigantic hand-carved columns of light grey wood. All was in red velvet accentuated by stained glass, ornamental iron work, murals, sculptures, antique furniture, and tropical palms and plants and vines. It was the perfect setting for formal teas, afternoon and nightly dancing, and Sunday religious services. The interior decorations were real works of art - not the trendy Art Deco, but instead Rococo, Roman Beaux Arts, even Feudal. There was practically no difference between the two sisters' construction or decoration except that the colour red dominated on the *Saturnia* and green on the *Vulcania*. The ships were also famed for the large number of staterooms that had private verandahs and private baths."

On a late 1930's voyage, Dr. McLean especially remembers, "The 'Captain's Get-together' and 'Farewell' dinners were most unusual - family names were printed on the menus and a few items you really liked were added as a specialty for you. Irving Berlin was at the table next to ours."

In the early years of the War, the *Saturnia* and *Vulcania* were laid-up mostly. Their American sailings ceased in the Spring of 1940, just as Italy entered the War as an axis power. Later, they made a few troop sailings with Italian soldiers over to North Africa and later still, in 1942, the *Saturnia* was briefly loaned to the International Red Cross for evacuation voyages out of East Africa. Both ships fled for safety, in early September of 1943, following Italy's capitulation. Both fell into American hands - the *Saturnia* eventually became the US Navy hospital ship *Frances Y. Slanger*, the *Vulcania* serving as an army transport. In Spring 1946, with the War over, the *Vulcania* made several passenger voyages on charter to the American Export Lines, sailing between New York and Italy and as far east as Alexandria. Then, with their American duties complete, they were handed back to the Italians in December 1946.

Quickly restored, the *Saturnia* reopened Italian Line's Naples-Genoa-New York service in January 1947. Her quarters were vastly restyled, however, to new, post-war standards - 240 in first class, 270 cabin class and then 860 in tourist class. The *Vulcania* was back six months later, in July, and briefly re-opened the old East Coast of South America service. She then went on the New York run as well a few months later.

"We had lots of Germans in the office then, all left over from the North German Lloyd and Hamburg America Line offices from 1939. You almost had to speak German to advance," according to Vito Matti, who worked for the American Export Lines in 1950. Their Lower New York City offices at 29 Broadway, then the very heart of 'Steamship Row', were the agents for the Italian Line and so booked passengers on the *Saturnia* and *Vulcania*. "We handled seven passenger ships altogether at the time - Export's 'Four Aces' (*Excalibur*, *Excambion*, *Exeter* and *Exochorda*), the *La Guardia* (a converted wartime troopship) and the two Italians. The Italian Line did not have its own, separate office untill 1952 - 53, when the brand new *Andrea Doria* first arrived. But in 1950, all the attention and excitement at American Export focused on the first brand new luxury liners for the Mediterranean since the War, the *Independence* and the *Constitution*."

Noted maritime author, artist and lecturer Frank Braynard, then a New York harbor marine reporter, went aboard the *Vulcania* in the late 1940s for a celebratory, return-to-service luncheon. "The dining room had to be one of the great shipboard achievements. It was completely restored. The ship was as she had been - stained glass windows, wood carvings, gilt cherubs and all. It was fantastic! I had always sort of discounted her with that stump funnel, but after that I reappraised her as one of the best liners afloat."

"The *Vulcania* was the very best passenger ship I ever worked", added Captain Renato Piovino, who served in her as a junior officer in the 1950s and early '60s. "She had been built to very high standards by the Cosulich family. She was very, very elegant. The first class corridors, for example, were all rosewood and there was an alabaster stairway. She was also an excellent 'sea boat', very stable - she didn't need stabilizers. There was great loyalty to the *Vulcania* by both passengers and crew. One New York family made 22 trips in her. I was aboard when the dresses for the film 'Cleopatra' were brought from New York to Naples in the *Vulcania*."

In 1953-54, when the brand new *Andrea Doria* and *Cristoforo Colombo* came into service and took over the express run out of Naples and Genoa, the *Saturnia* and the *Vulcania* returned to the Adriatic. They were routed on five and six week round voyages: Trieste, Venice, Dubrovnik, Patras, Messina and / or Palermo, Naples, Gibraltar, Lisbon, Halifax (west-bound only) and then New York. They returned often via Boston and Ponta Delgada in the Azores, Lisbon, Gibraltar, Palermo, Naples, Patras, Venice and Trieste. The same fares to Lisbon applied to Venice and so, according to Professor McLean, "It was a 15- or 20-day Mediterranean Sea cruise for the price of a regular 5-day crossing. We called at 8 ports and could get off for sightseeing at all."

"We landed tens of thousands of immigrants from Italy, Greece and Portugal at Halifax, " recalled Giancarlo Roccatagliata, a waiter who served aboard both ships. "In 1956, in particular, we brought many Hungarians to Halifax. They were escaping the Communist takeover in their homeland.

"On many trips, we might have as many as 1,500 passengers onboard, but we would land 1,000 at Halifax and then bring the remaining 500 to New York. We would also sell the 2 - day passages down from Halifax to New York for about $20. I also remember that it was very, very cold at Halifax in winter. Often, the *Saturnia* and *Vulcania* would be completely covered in ice. We used buckets of hot water to melt it. "

The *Saturnia* and *Vulcania* sailed for the Italian Line until April 1965, the same year the giant *Michelangelo* and *Raffaello* came into service. There was a fleet reshuffling and the *Cristoforo Colombo* was shifted to the Adriatic as their replacement. Moored together for some time at Trieste, the *Saturnia* was subsequently sold to Italian shipbreakers that October and broken-up at La Spezia. The *Vulcania* was sold for further service however, and while nearly forty, went to another Italian shipowner, the Siosa Lines. She resumed sailing in

Right: The stately home gone to sea: the splendid first class library aboard the *Vulcania,* shown in the late 1940s.
Below: Post-war splendor: The first class dining room aboard the *Saturnia* as seen in 1947.   *Both, Maurizio Eliseo collection*

February 1966 as the *Caribia*.

"The *Saturnia* was worn out by 1965 and so had to be scrapped, " noted Captain Piovino. "But *Vulcania* was in impeccable condition when she went to Siosa." The former *Vulcania*'s story is continued in the section on Grimaldi - Siosa Lines.

Resuming service in 1949, the *Conte Biancamano* and the *Conte Grande* (shown outbound from New York on September 8th 1956) restored the Italian Line's South American service to its pre-war standard. They ran from Naples, Genoa, Cannes, Barcelona, Lisbon and Dakar to Rio de Janeiro, Santos, Montevideo and Buenos Aires. The *Conte Biancamano* was also routed in peak summers, from 1950 until 1960, to help on the Naples-Genoa-New York run. The *Conte Grande* assisted also, but only for two voyages in 1956.

Flying Camera Inc.

The two Conti

Above: "Like the *Saturnia* and the *Vulcania*, the *Conte Biancamano* (shown arriving in New York on March 18th 1950) and the *Conte Grande* were very solid, very stable ships", according to Captain Fossati. "They had very good care while in American hands during the War". They too had been built in the 1920s - the *Conte Biancamano* came from the William Beardmore yard at Glasgow in 1925; the *Conte Grande* from Stabilimento Tecnico at Trieste in 1928. Both were built for Lloyd Sabaudo, the Genoa-based shipowner merged into the Italian Line in 1932. *Flying Camera Inc.*

Left: Unassisted by tugs during a strike, the *Conte Biancamano* cautiously makes her way into the south slip of Pier 84 at New York. The year is 1957.

Maurizio Eliseo collection

Right: "In first class to South America, ships like the *Conte Biancamano* and the *Conte Grande* carried rich Italians, Brazilians and Argentinians and the high Catholic clergy such as cardinals and bishops. Because we were State-owned, we always carried members of the Roman Church", noted Captain Fossati. In this example of post-war elegance and style, the modernised, greatly altered first class restaurant on board the *Conte Grande*.

Frank O. Braynard collection

Below: The first class swimming pool and lido area on board the *Conte Grande* was located between her twin funnels.

Frank O. Braynard collection

Passenger-cargo liners

Above: Just as the War was about to start for Italy in 1940, the Italian Line ordered six large cargo ships for its South American services. Three were launched in 1942, the others in 1945. They were later redesigned with more pressing post-war demands in mind and so were fitted with quarters for 90 in cabin class and as many as 530 in third class. They were completed in 1947-49 as the *Paolo Toscanelli, Ugolino Vivaldi, Sebastiano Caboto, Marco Polo, Amerigo Vespucci* and the *Antoniotto Usodimare* (shown sailing from Naples in 1953). They reopened Italian Line's post-war West Coast of South America service. Genoa all the way to Valparaiso in Chile took 30 days and sailings from Italy were just about monthly.   *Eric Johnson*

Below: In 1958, the *Paolo Toscanelli, Sebastiano Caboto* and *Ugolino Vivaldi* were downgraded to 12-passenger freighters; the *Amerigo Vespucci, Antoniotto Usodimare* and *Marco Polo* followed in 1963. Mostly, they went into freighter service for Lloyd Triestino (the *Ugolino Vivaldi* is shown at Cape Town) until all were scrapped by 1978.   *Alex Duncan*

The New Generation

Left: "The *Augustus* and the *Giulio Cesare (left)* were unusually big motorliners - 27,000 tons each and Fiat had a very special interest in them", according to Captain Fossati. "Fiat technicians and engineers inspected each ship following every round voyage. Actually, their diesels were built just before the War, in 1939, and then kept in storage until the early 1950s. When the plans for these ships were first drawn in 1948, someone remembered these engines. They were the largest Fiat diesels yet fitted to passenger ships. The *Augustus* and the *Giulio Cesare* were built with post-war American financial aid".

Luis Miguel Correia

The *Augustus* (above) and the *Giulio Cesare* sailed in year-round service to the East Coast of South America until June 1956, when the *Giulio Cesare* was re-routed to New York for peak summer sailings. A month later, the *Andrea Doria* would sink and so her presence became especially important. The *Augustus* joined the New York run in February 1957 and in due course made 40 round voyages on the North Atlantic. The *Cesare* reverted to full-time Latin American service in 1960, the *Augustus* a year later. "These ships actually earned a double profit for some years - Latin America in winter, New York in the equally busy summers", according to Captain Fossati. The *Augustus* is shown leaving New York in 1957 with the *Ocean Monarch, Queen of Bermuda* and *Gripsholm* in the background.

Flying Camera Inc.

Genova di notte - I supertransatlantici "Augustus" e "Andrea Doria" in Porto

Above: The *Augustus* and the *Giulio Cesare* carried tens of thousands of emigrants to South America and then returned with low-fare tourists to Europe. Giancarlo Roccatagliata recalled a rather special *Augustus* east-bound passage in 1967: "We had lots of Jewish passengers going from Argentina to Israel via Italy. We had to divide the galley - half-Italian, half-Kosher. Everything had to be specially cooked for those Orthodox passengers". In this view, the *Augustus* is shown at Genoa with the *Andrea Doria* in the background.

Everett Viez collection

Below: The first class lounge aboard the *Augustus* in 1951 was in marked contrast to the more ornate styles often used on Italian ships in the 1920s and 1930s.

Frank O. Braynard collection

Right: The *Giulio Cesare* developed mechanical difficulties and then rudder trouble in 1972. She is shown awaiting the breakers at La Spezia the following year. *Antonio Scrimali*

14

Last Of The Italian Line

The *Augustus* was not retired from Italian Line service until January 1976, the very twilight of that once great company's passenger operations. At first she was laid-up at Naples. She too might have been scrapped, but instead found further life - but not necessarily further employment - in distant Far Eastern waters. The ship was sold to Great Shipping & Investments Limited, registered under the flag of the Seychelles and named *Great Sea*. She was moved to Hong Kong, supposedly for repairs and reconditioning. Within less than a year, she changed to Panamanian registry. Barely ever leaving her Hong Kong moorings, she was sold, in 1980, to the Ocean King Navigation Company of Manila and renamed *Ocean King*. Two years later, she was moved to an anchorage at that capital city and later to Subic Bay, and in the following year was restyled as the accommodation ship *Philippines* (some reports suggest it was spelled *Philipinas*). In 1985, she was renamed yet again, this time as the *President*. In 1987, she became the *Asian Princess*, first registered at Hong Kong and then back to Manila. She moved to Keelung for further lay-up. Exact details and even her precise whereabouts have often been clouded in mystery. In the Spring of 1986, for example, several American newspapers reported that she was a 'treasure ship' filled with artworks, antiques and other valuable items that supposedly belonged to ex-President Marcos and his wife Imelda.

Scott Baty, an Australian cruise specialist and author of a book on Pacific Ocean liners, visited the former *Augustus* at about the same time, in 1986: "I saw her at Subic Bay, and was invited to have a short, private cruise in her. She was owned by the Yap family, who also owned the Philippine President Lines, the country's largest cargo carrier. No one seemed to be sure why they had actually bought the ship, but at one point they wanted to start a South Pacific cruise service out of Brisbane with her."

"Structurally, she was much the same as originally built, but her passenger quarters had been remodelled in Filipino styles. There seemed to be velvet everywhere and in reds, oranges and lime green! The former Belvedere Lounge had been converted to a large owner's suite. It had beds with covered headboards.

The *Great Sea*, the former *Augustus*, is shown anchored at Hong Kong in April 1979.   *Steffen Weirauch*

The former first class restaurant had been redone as the Luzon Room and the old tourist class dining room as the Zamboanga Room."

"At the time of my visit, there were rumours that she might be sold to the Chinese," Mr. Baty recalled, "but this never materialized. Also, it seems that in the summer of 1983, while laid-up at Hong Kong, the former *Augustus* was moored alongside one of her old Italian Line fleetmates, the *Cristoforo Colombo*. That ship was soon towed across to Taiwan and scrapped. But the saga of the *Augustus* continues."

The legendary Andrea Doria

After a 'shakedown' cruise to the Canary Islands, the 700-foot long *Andrea Doria* left Genoa in January 1953 on her first crossing to New York. "The *Andrea Doria* and her later sister, the *Cristoforo Colombo*, were especially luxurious, built for the high demands of the American trade", recalled Captain Fossati. "We often carried celebrities - such as Ambassador Clare Booth Luce and Hollywood stars like Clark Gable and Elizabeth Taylor. And unlike the earlier motorliners in our fleet, both of these ships needed steam turbines so as to have greater service speeds - at least 23 knots".

Richard C. Faber collection

Above: "The best and most important Italian artists and artisans decorated these two great Italian liners", according to Captain Piovino. "First class was especially magnificent. Even the doorknobs were works of art. I always thought the *Colombo* (on the left) had the very best quality. As an officer to serve on these ships, we had to know at least two languages other than Italian and we were expected to dance with the first class passengers each evening. The Italian Line ran three separate training schools, which provided the staff for these ships and our other big liners".

Right: The magnificent *Andrea Doria* in drydock at Naples in 1955. On another occasion, Michelangelo's 'Pieta' was sent to New York for the 1964 World's Fair aboard the *Cristoforo Colombo*. "This was our most precious cargo and we even put the *Colombo* in drydock at Naples so she wouldn't move during the very careful loading process", remembered Captain Fossati. "A big crane was used for the specially made case that was filled with plastic foam. It was lowered on a rubber base that was placed in the first class pool. This case was especially 'floatable' in case of sinking. It could be released quite easily with snap hooks". *Both, Richard C. Faber collection*

The Andrea Doria Revisited

In July 1956, when just over three years old, the *Andrea Doria* made her biggest headlines. Ever since, she has retained a sort of maritime immortality. Inbound from Genoa to New York, on a foggy night off Nantucket Island, Italy's pride and joy was rammed by the Swedish-American liner *Stockholm*. The Swede was a smaller ship but the blow proved fatal to the big

Sad ending: The magnificent *Andrea Doria* sinking off Nantucket Island in the early morning hours of July 26th 1956.

Richard C. Faber collection

Italian. In the first daylight hours of the next morning, July 26, the abandoned 700-foot liner rolled over and then slipped under the Atlantic waves forever. Now resting in her underwater grave for nearly forty years, Dr. David Bright makes regular visits to the remains of the Italian Line flagship. A specialist diver from New Jersey, Dr Bright has a particular fascination for passenger ship and passenger ship-related wrecks.

"The *Andrea Dodia* is 245 feet from the surface," according to Dr Bright, "and well encrusted in the sand. Comparatively, another liner, Canadian Pacific's *Empress of Ireland*, which sank in the St Lawrence, rests in 165 feet of water. The Cunard *Lusitania*, which was torpedoed in 1915 off the south-eastern coast of Ireland, is down 315 feet. White Star's *Britannic*, mined in the Aegean in 1916, is the deepest of these, at 390 feet."

"When I first visited the *Doria*'s remains in the summer of 1987, I concentrated on the bow section, but then also noticed that the top three decks had slipped off. The mast and the funnel were gone as well. Certainly, they are lying down there somewhere. Some divers say that storms have done this, but others claim it was a Russian trawler dragging huge nets. In the wreckage, there were all sorts of scattered objects. That summer, for example, I found a medicine bottle, completely intact. It has since been bought by E.R. Squibb & Sons, the pharmaceutical giant of Princeton, New Jersey, and is now in their corporate museum."

"The *Doria* is the most deadly of all famous wrecks, however," added Dr Bright. "You must know the ship's plan by heart, especially since many walls are gone and then there's lots and lots of silt. It's like a cave. You can be trapped so easily. There are masses of nylon fishing nets, often containing trapped dead fish. The electrical cables are also very dangerous to divers. So many ceilings have collapsed and there are wires everywhere. With the muck, you can swim right into these cables. It's like swimming into the clutches of an octupus. The *Andrea Doria* is very, very dangerous."

David Bright has also visited the remains of another liner, White Star's 15,300-ton *Republic*, built in 1903 and then sunk six years later after colliding with the Italian *Florida*. The *Republic* is one of the *Doria*'s neighbours in that darkened underwater world. "The *Republic* is about 5 miles away from the *Andrea Doria*," according to Dr Bright: "She rests in about 260 feet of water. Loaded with a shipment of gold bullion when she sank, she is now in a very poor condition. There had been lots of ripping at her by earlier divers to get that gold."

"The *Andrea Doria* remains of very great interest within the ocean liner collectible market," according to Richard Faber, a New York-based dealer: "Part of the reason is the dramatic circumstances of her demise. Disasters are especially fascinating to collectors, but the *Doria* was unusual in being lost after a collision with another liner. Rather strangely, however, there is

In this scene from New York dated September 26th 1956, the *Cristoforo Colombo* is at Pier 84, at the foot of West 44th Street. Also included are the *America, United States, Alsatia* and the *Queen Elizabeth*.   *Flying Camera Inc.*

absolutely no appeal for collectors on the *Stockholm*. Also, of course, the *Andrea Doria* was a great beauty. She has many admirers. A porcelain souvenir ashtray, sold in the gift shop onboard, today fetches $150. A first class menu can go for $40, a glass from the first class service might also be $40 and a photo postcard of the *Doria* can be as much as $25. And very recently, the *Cristoforo Colombo* is coming into her own in the collectors market as well. Sisterships, such as the *Olympic* to the *Titanic*, are more and more popular."

Passing in mid-Atlantic was something of an Italian Line tradition. The *Cristoforo Colombo* is seen from the *Conte Biancamano* (*Richard C. Faber collection*) while the photograph of the *Conte Grande* was taken from the *Giulio Cesare*.   *Antonio Scrimali*

Above: After the loss of the *Doria*, the *Colombo* was later paired with the larger *Leonardo Da Vinci*. In 1965, she was reassigned to the longer route from the Adriatic, replacing the *Saturnia* and the *Vulcania*. In 1973, she was moved onto the East Coast of South America run until retired in 1977.   *Port Authority of New York & New Jersey*

Below: In April 1977, the *Cristoforo Colombo* was sold to the Venezuelan Government for $7 million. Shortly thereafter, she left Genoa for Mantanzas in the Orinoco Estuary to take up her role as a permanently moored workers' accommodation centre. She would service a local steel plant. Then, in 1980, she was sold again, this time to Taiwanese scrappers. Towed across the Pacific, she was delivered at Kaohsiung on 30th June 1981. Her scrapyard owners felt that they might get even more money on the resale market and so moved her to Hong Kong for more convenient inspection by prospective buyers. Unfortunately, there were no takers. In July 1983, she returned to Kaohsiung and was then scrapped. Barely noticed, the era of the great post-war Italian Line passenger ships was just about gone completely.   *Steffen Weirauch collection*

Remembering the Da Vinci

Just weeks after the luxurious *Andrea Doria* plunged to the bottom of the western Atlantic off Nantucket on that summer's night in 1956, her Italian Line owners summoned their naval architects. They called for designs for a replacement, for a liner that would be equally splendid and noteworthy. She would be the new national flagship. She would be christened the *Leonardo Da Vinci.*

The 761-foot long liner, built at the Ansaldo yard at Genoa and finally completed in June 1960, was a stunning-looking ship. Her overall design was clearly

in tourist. 1960 fares for eight to nine day crossings from New York to Naples and Genoa ranged from $390 in first class to $235 in tourist.

But like most ships, the 23-knot *Da Vinci* did have her blemishes. "She had a stability problem," remembered Captain Fossati, her one time master. "We had to put 3,000 tons of iron in her double bottoms just to steady her. Thereafter, being heavier, she had a very high fuel consumption rate. She was always an expensive ship to operate and certainly far less profitable than her Italian Government sponsors would have liked."

In addition to her regular mid-Atlantic crossings, the *Da Vinci* also ran an annual eight week wintertime

Generally considered to be one of Italy's finest-looking passenger liners, the *Leonardo Da Vinci* in her maiden year, 1960.

Roger Sherlock

a development of successive Italian liners, each of them very handsome and very contemporary. But the 33,300-ton *Da Vinci* included improvements as well, such as the aft cargo space on the earlier ships being used instead as a larger lido area, which included no less than six swimming pools - three for adults and three for children. Mechanically, it was widely publicized that she would be easily convertible from steam turbines to nuclear power. A conversion might come, according to one Italian Line publicist, as early as 1965. Internally, she had some splendid public rooms and far more private plumbing in her cabins, including as much as 80% in the otherwise usually austere tourist class section. Overall, the *Da Vinci* could carry 1,326 passengers - 413 in first class, 342 in cabin class and 571

Mediterranean-Black Sea cruise and later sailed the Caribbean and to South America. In 1970, she made an unusual cruise from New York to Hawaii, sailing via the Panama Canal. On that trip, she carried many passengers who had been booked aboard the "Great Pacific Cruise" scheduled for the superliner *United States* that January. Also operating in the red, that famed ship was abruptly withdrawn from service two months before, in November 1969. Her US Government benefactors were no longer interested in supporting her money-losing operations. The same fate would later befall the *Da Vinci* and her Italian Line fleetmates.

"We always seemed to have notable passengers aboard the *Da Vinci*," added Giancarlo Roccatagliata, a

Italian Line celebrity passengers: King Ibn Saud of Saudi Arabia - and film queen Gloria Swanson.   *Victor Rollo collection*

former maitre'd on board. "On the Mediterranean crossings, we'd always have Hollywood celebrities. I recall Paul Newman, Gloria Swanson, Zachary Scott, Joan Fontaine, Tony Curtis and Janet Leigh. I especially remember Gloria Swanson bringing along lots of her own health foods and all of her own mineral water. We also had Elizabeth Taylor and Richard Burton. He was great fun, but Miss Taylor wanted lots of privacy and even used the crew stairwells when going to and from the first class restaurant. I also recall Spencer Tracy, Charlton Heston, Gore Vidal, Prince Rainier and Princess Grace of Monaco, and lots of Catholic hierarchy - the cardinals and the archbishops and their entourages."

"I remember that Salvador Dali booked a separate cabin just for his pet ocelots," added Roccatagliata. "The butcher prepared special meats and other foods just for them. We also had Yugoslavia's President Tito and his wife, going from New York to Italy. There was a huge police guard at Pier 84 for the sailing. His security forces feared the Yugoslav dockworkers. There were even scuba divers checking for bombs. Tito travelled with ten security men. He spent a great deal of time walking around the ship, but with at least four of them always in close attendance. They were always armed. Tito and his party sat at a table for twelve in the dining room. But surprisingly, no one ever checked the food. Instead, they seemed more concerned with the other passengers."

The *Da Vinci* also endured what Roccatagliata called "evil" North Atlantic weather. "The worst storm I recall lasted three days. Everyone just stayed on the lounge floors. We served them sandwiches and fruit. The ship was rolling constantly. We were only going three miles per hour, but we were really sort of drifting. Everyone was too frightened to get seasick."

Joined by the larger, splashier pair of *Michelangelo* and *Raffaello* in 1965, the *Da Vinci* soon became a sort of 'second fiddle' and then began to fall on hard times. In the end, by 1976, she closed out the entire Italian Line trans-Atlantic service altogether. A year later, in a bid largely to keep Italian seamen employed, she was used on the Miami-Nassau overnight run for the newly

created Italian Line Cruises International, but was actually managed by the Costa Line. But the sparkle was long gone. One captain bitterly reported, "The *Da Vinci* still burned more fuel at dock than most ships do at sea."

Laid-up at La Spezia, in September 1977, she would never sail again. Expectedly, she was the subject of enormous and usually erroneous rumors. Would she be moored in the Thames as a casino or rebuilt as a luxury cruiseship charging as much as $200 a day? Nothing came to pass until July 4, 1980, when still laid-up, barely guarded and just stripped of her valuable art collection, she caught fire. It all started in the chapel and then spread, raging for four days. Thousands flocked to the shoreline to witness her fiery end. It all ended outside harbor waters where she was left half-submerged in forty feet of water and with a sixty degree list. With a scrap value of just over $2 million but with an insurance appraisal of nearly $8 million, her charred remains were finally cut-up two years later. What a very sad ending for the great *Leonardo Da Vinci*.

Goddess in ashes: The burnt-out wreckage of the *Leonardo Da Vinci* lying on its side at La Spezia in July 1980.

Antonio Scrimali

The salvaged remains of the *Da Vinci*......

and the once great ship being broken up.   *Antonio Scrimali*

Below: With the Italian Line wanting to improve its Italy-West coast of South America service and then with Lloyd Triestino taking on their brand new *Guglielmo Marconi* and *Galileo Galilei,* there was a 'swap' within the controlling Finmare Group. The 1951-built trio of *Australia, Neptunia* and *Oceania,* which had maintained Lloyd Triestino's Australian service for over a decade, went to the Italian Line in 1963. They became the 'Three Musicians' - the *Donizetti, Rossini* and the *Verdi. (Alex Duncan) Left:* Fares for the 30-day voyage from Italy to Chile in 1963 were $600 in first and $380 in tourist class. Rino Rivieccio was assistant purser aboard the *Rossini (left)* in 1971. "We carried not only Italian, but French and Spanish passengers as well. We also had rich Central and South Americans. The immigrants in tourist class sailed mostly to Venezuela. Just a few went to West Coast ports. Of course, cargo was also very important. We carried general cargo outwards; homebound, we loaded cotton in Chile and carried metals and sometimes coffee". Retired in 1976, the 'Three Musicians' then went to the breakers at La Spezia.   *Roger Sherlock*

The Italian Superliners

"The *Michelangelo* and *Raffaello* often used to pass one another at sea, in mid-Atlantic, and this always caused lots of excitement," recalled Giancarlo Roccatagliata, a former maitre'd onboard these ships. "There would be horns blowing and balloons and flares and lots of waving. It was kind of a great show. The ships would be travelling in opposite directions at combined speeds of well over 50 knots!"

Completed in 1965, the 45,900-ton ships were built (the *Michelangelo* at Ansaldo's Genoa yards, the *Raffaello* at Cantieri Riuniti dell'Adriatico at Monfalcone) for the Italian Line's express run between Naples, Genoa, Cannes, Algeciras and NewYork. So enthused were New York officials that they offered to demolish some old railroad piers just north of "Luxury Liner Row" at West 66th Street and build a new passenger terminal especially for the Italian Line. They proposed a squared facility with three berths similar to Holland

Queen Elizabeth. It made for interesting contrasts in passenger ship design and development. "But these sister ships were actually already too late for the trans-Atlantic trade. Already, passengers were taking planes," noted Roccatagliata. "But the Government had to build them under pressure from several very powerful Italian unions. They gave work to the shipyards, to the dockers and especially to the seamen. At first, they were planned to be smaller ships, at 35,000 tons each and so just a little bigger than the *Leonardo Da Vinci*, but work was stopped and the plans changed. They were great ships in many ways, but not successful financially. As cruiseships, we could not use 700 or so berths in tourist class because those cabins were too small and too austere. This too cut into their profits."

"Actually, the Government-owned Italian Line never had a ship that was ideally suited for cruising," added

Spanking new, the *Michelangelo* prepares for her May 1965 maiden voyage at Genoa.   *Schiffsfotos Jansen*

America Line's new Pier 40. An artist's rendering referred to the project as "Italian Line's Pier 99." In fact, beginning in late 1963, the Italian Line took over the lease on Cunard's Pier 90, at West 50th Street, which had been built in 1936 for the maiden arrival of the *Queen Mary*. Now in decline, Cunard needed only to maintain a single terminal at New York, adjacent Pier 92. And so, these sleek Italian beauties with their long white hulls, raked bows and birdcage-like stacks shared the same slip with the *Queen Mary* and the

Roccatagliata. "All of them were traditionally class-divided ships, not easily made over for week long runs to the Caribbean. We experimented with longer cruises as well - to the Black Sea and the Holy Land, Carnival-in-Rio and even up to the North Cape from Genoa. I remember that on one North Cape trip, we had ten American passengers onboard amongst 600 or so Italians."

The 1,775 passenger *Michelangelo* and *Raffaello* were big and beautiful, but increasingly expensive. In the

A large model of the *Michelangelo* sits before the actual ship under construction at the Ansaldo yard at Genoa in 1964.

Richard C. Faber collection

The *Raffaello*, on the right and dressed in flags, prepares for her maiden voyage to New York in July 1965. In this aerial view at Genoa, the *Michelangelo* and Lauro Lines' *Roma* are to the left while the *Augustus* is being towed to the outer harbor.

Willie Tinnemeyer collection

end, they were subsidized by the Ministry of Marine Transport at a rate that made scandalously embarrassing headlines in Italian newspapers. "Sometimes, in winter on the North Atlantic, we would have more crew than passengers," added Roccatagliata. "And sometimes more crew were sick than passengers. In rough weather, ropes were strung about and the portholes were covered. But sometimes, the portholes would break. The *Michelangelo* was hit by a massive wave (in April 1966) that caused tremendous damage to her forward superstructure. Afterward, both ships needed to be reinforced, to have stronger upper-deck construction. Actually, at sea, the *Michelangelo* and the *Raffaello* were not as flexible as our older, smaller liners. They were too rigid. Older ships like the *Saturnia* and the *Vulcania* had low bows and so entered the waves whereas these newer ships had great flared bows and so tended to collide with high waves."

Myself, I recall crossing on the *Raffaello* in the summer of 1973, from Naples to New York on a ten day passage that was part of a so-called "Mediterranean Go-Round" cruise. We had full day calls at Genoa, Cannes, Barcelona, Gibraltar/Algeciras and finally Lisbon. It was $600 for a two berth room in cabin class. The other passengers were interesting, the service still very good and the pasta flawless. At Cannes, I especially recall the barge-tender coming alongside and then off-loading some mighty Cadillacs and Rolls Royces into the forward holds, and later some of those big, brown, well-labelled Vuitton trunks. That night, there was a gala fireworks extravaganza sponsored by the Red Chinese Government. The 902-foot long *Raffaello* sat, with all of her lights temporarily switched off, as multi-colored flashes and sprays soared around her. When we finally reached New York's Pier 86, the *Michelangelo* arrived an hour before us, inbound from a Caribbean cruise. This great $120 million pair of mighty Italians were together on one of the very few occasions at New York. But within two years, by the summer of 1975, the Italian Government withdrew its vital support and so the sisters were finished.

Vincent Messina, a former staff member aboard cruiseships and a veteran of several hundred voyages, was aboard the *Michelangelo* for one of her west bound crossings, also in 1973. "I was travelling in tourist class, which was now combined with the old cabin class. It was dreadful! The cabin was small, the shower even smaller and the bed sheets not changed once in nine days! The apathy of the crew was magnified in tourist class. They were indifferent to all."

"There was only fifteen minutes 'grace' in the dining room," added Messina. "After that, you were locked

Above: The spectacular first class ballroom aboard the *Michelangelo*.
Below: The first class lounge aboard the *Raffaello*.

Both, Frank O. Braynard collection

Above: The first class hall aboard the *Raffaello*.

Frank O. Braynard collection

1960s luxury: *Above:* The first class ballroom and *right* the first class dining room aboard *Michelangelo*.

Richard C. Faber collection

Above: A deck scene aboard *Michelangelo.*

Richard C. Faber collection

Below: The *Raffaello* (left) and the *Michelangelo,* laid-up and 'nested together' at La Spezia in the fall of 1975.

Antonio Scrimali

out! There was scummy red table wine in a dirty carafe. During the day, the class barriers were relaxed, but at night they came down like an iron grill. Physically, they were marvellous ships, the deck space was great and the first and cabin class public rooms quite beautiful. Once in New York harbor, I saw many Italian immigrants cry as we sailed past the Statue of Liberty."

But in the very end, these and other Italian Line passenger ships were plagued with another major problem: strikes. "There were lots of strikes, for 24 and 48 hours, and then too many of them and for any silly reason," concluded Giancarlo Roccatagliata. "Once there was a strike simply because the ship ran out of mineral water for the crew. In the end, in 1975-76, they pushed the Italian Line and the Government to close out all passenger service."

"Rome suddenly cut almost all passenger liner subsidies in 1975," recalled Captain Piovino. "There had been a tremendous decline of passengers. Ships like the *Michelangelo* and *Raffaello* were losing too much money and were certainly too expensive to operate. Thousands were suddenly out of work. Many staff went into early retirement and many to cargo ships. Lots of Italian Line personnel found jobs with Sitmar, Costa, Princess Cruises, Home Lines and with Carnival Cruise Lines. Seven former Italian Line captains joined Carnival." Himself, Captain Piovino went on to become master of Carnival's *Mardi Gras*, the *Carnivale* and the

In the summer of 1977, the *Michelangelo* was in more distant waters - moored in the harbor of Bandar Abbas, Iran.

William Fox collection

Festivale. Captain Fossati, who also joined Carnival and commanded the *Mardi Gras*, the *Festivale* and the *Tropicale*, was assigned to the decommissioning of the *Michelangelo* and *Raffaello*. "They were highly unprofitable ships. Actually, they were kept in service until the very last moment. After their last crossings (the *Raffaello* in April 1975, the *Michelangelo* three months later), we kept them at Genoa for a few months and then, in September, moved them to Porto Venere in the Gulf of La Spezia. We moored them side-by-side, but in reverse. This gave us anchors at each end. Everything was stripped. A crew of fifty moved all the art, carpets, even the china and the glassware ashore to warehouses. But we were specially instructed to leave all the instruments on the bridge."

Stripping these Italian liners upon retirement had become a rather common practice. Because they were State-owned ships, their passenger fittings, particularly their art treasures, found their way into Government offices, other State businesses and even private homes. The art from the *Giulio Cesare*, for example, was divided-up and some went to a Milanese bank. Pieces from the *Leonardo Da Vinci* later found their way into various Government offices in Rome. Smaller items, however, were placed in the basement of the Italian Line's Genoa home office until, in the mid-1980s, that property was closed and sold. Unfortunately, this archive finished up in Government incinerators.

Rino Rivieccio, one time chief purser on both the *Michelangelo* and the *Raffaello*, went aboard the laid-up giants at La Spezia in late 1975. "It was like seeing a person dying. Only a watchman was aboard. There were very few lights. The china, the linen, the carpets and all the artwork were gone. Only the furniture remained. There were nets over the swimming pools. It was all very quiet, not a sound. It was haunting. There weren't even flags at the mast. The two ships were moored together for strength. There were rumours that they would soon be scrapped on the nearby beaches at La Spezia."

While it was rumoured that a Liechtenstein-based organisation wanted to make them over as floating cancer research and recovery clinics which would run two and three week Mediterranean cruises, other companies inspected the legendary pair. Costa Line thought they would be too expensive to operate and so did Norwegian Caribbean Lines. Chandris was interested, but was then more concerned about the decline of its own Australian migrant trade and just could not see them as full time cruiseships. The Soviets also had a look and so did C.Y. Tung, and there was a South American firm that wanted them for low cost housing. But it was the Iranians who got the idle pair in the end.

In an oil swap deal with Italy, the Shah of Iran's government took them for use as military barracks. They went through Suez to their new homes in 1977 - the *Michelangelo* to Bandar Abbas, the *Raffaello* to Bushire. Afterward, army officers and cadets piled aboard. There was, however, a rather lengthy plan

The last remains of the *Michelangelo* being broken-up by the firm of Ghaffar Dada at Gadani Beach, Pakistan on November 9th 1991.
Gregory Vossos

drawn up in 1978 that proposed they be restyled and refitted as luxury cruise ships. While still Iranian owned, they would fly a flag-of-convenience and sail Mediterranean and Caribbean waters with reduced capacities of about 1,300 each. They were to be renamed *Reza Shah The Great* and *Cyrus The Great*.

Captain Fossati went to Iran in 1978 as part of a cooperative arrangement between Italy and Iran. "There were fifty Italians onboard for maintenance as well as advisory purposes. But already, they were in very, very poor condition. It was clear that they would never sail again."

They also housed American technicians working in Iran on oil company contracts, but the ships fell further into disrepair. Their hulls gathered more and more rust, the outer decks began to buckle and - worst of all - they were invaded by armies of rats!

The *Raffaello* was bombed and then sunk in an Iraqi air attack on Bushire in February 1983. Her remains barely poked above the harbour waters. Four years later, on February 4, 1987, the 9,200 ton Iranian freighter *Iran Salam* went aground at Bushire and was badly damaged. This incident would have been quite ordinary, in fact almost unnoticed, except that she grounded on the sunken wreckage of the former *Raffaello*. There were later reports that she was to be salvaged, repaired and offered to foreign buyers, but this never came to pass. Meanwhile, the *Michelangelo* lingered, caught in a veil of both mystery and rumor. She was to have been sold to Florida's Premier Cruise Lines for probable short cruises to the Bahamas and then it was reported that she was scrapped at Kaohsiung, Taiwan in 1988, but both reports proved false. She was, however, sold to Pakistani scrap

merchants in the summer of 1991.

Gadani Beach, a six mile stretch of sand between a desert and the Arabian Sea, is but a dot on the map of Pakistan. It is an hour's drive from Karachi, the bustling capital city. Gadani Beach is not a tourist mecca or even especially well known to the Pakistanis themselves. But it is something of an industrial hub: it is the home to one of the biggest and busiest ship-dismantling facilities anywhere. Over 6,000 ships (by 1991) - from supertankers to oil rigs, from vintage tramps to old Soviet subs - have ended their days there since the early 1970s.

Among the "dead ships" that dropped their final anchors there and then were systematically run onto the beach as they were "chewed up" by groups of yellow-robed men with acetylene torches, axes and hammers was the former *Michelangelo*. By then twenty six years old, the former luxury ship was a sad, very rusted, almost unrecognizable sight as she arrived at Gadani Beach in July 1991. She was by far the biggest passenger ship yet dismantled there.

It took six months to scrap the *Michelangelo*. The work was done entirely by Pathan tribesmen, mountain people who have become experts in ship demolition. They work twelve hours a day, seven days a week and, in 1991, earned a princely $10 a day, a decent wage by the then current Pakistani standards. In all, the *Michelangelo* yielded over $1 million in scrap metal. Throughout 1992, her remains still lined the cluttered beach: engine room parts, her wheelhouse equipment, even stacks of Milanese-made toilets. Smaller fittings, like bathroom light fixtures and kitchen pots, found their way to the back streets of Karachi. These were the "last rites" of the once grand *Michelangelo*.

Chapter Two

Lloyd Triestino

Lloyd Triestino, started in 1837, is said to be the oldest shipping company in the world. (Very close, Cunard was formed three years later.) Until recently housed in a grand palazzo at Trieste that was more like a museum than an active shipping office (there were enormous oil paintings, highly detailed models and gleaming brass nautical fixtures), the company is now headquartered in a modern office building. Today Lloyd Triestino has a fleet of very modern container-cargo ships. But they were once a great passenger line as well.

"We had passenger ships until the early 1980s", noted Captain Lorenzo Calvillo, who began sailing for Lloyd Triestino in 1957. In the 1950s, the line had seven passenger ships, all impeccably white, exquisitely served and fed, and trading out of the Mediterranean to Africa, Australia and the Far East. They made ideal connections for the bigger Italian Line ships that crossed to and from New York. In fact, the Italian Line represented Lloyd Triestino (along with several other Italian passenger firms) in their Lower Manhattan offices on State Street and, later, on Whitehall Street.

"My first big passenger ship was the *Asia*, which sailed between Italy, India and Hong Kong," remembered the Captain. "We had mostly British passengers back in the '50s and German and Swiss business people. There were also Eastern merchants, the clergy and missionaries, and the odd sultan, who usually took three or four cabins and brought along his own servants and bodyguards. On the three week trips out to Hong Kong, we also had lots of cargo - Italian dresses, leather shoes and auto parts going out. Home to Italy, we carried mostly inexpensive goods made in Japan but trans-shipped to Hong Kong. These included toys, plastic umbrellas, the little novelties."

The 11,500-ton *Africa* was the Captain's next assignment, sailing down to East and then South African ports. "A beautiful ship that handled very well in even the worst weather, we treated her and her sister, the *Europa,* like new brides. There were lots of diplomats and civil servants onboard in those years. The airplane was not yet a threat. Once, we had Mussolini's daughter Edda onboard. She had a farm in Kenya. She bought lots of things from the vendors at Port Said, just before we entered the Suez Canal. I brought them to her stateroom and she rewarded me with a yellow rose, which I actually kept until very recently. We also called at Mogadishu in Somalia, once an Italian territory. We anchored offshore and used to take on and discharge our passengers, three or four at a time, in big, round, canvas baskets called 'mamicias'. Cargo cranes on deck did the lifting and lowering."

The 9,584-ton *Toscana* was Lloyd Triestino's only surviving passenger ship after the Second World War. She had been North German Lloyd's *Saarbrucken* , built in 1923 for the Bremerhaven-Suez-Far East run. The Italians bought her in 1935 and then, after the War, she spent twelve years on the Italy-Australia route. She carried 819 all-third class passengers. The old ship was finally laid-up at Genoa in 1960 and then demolished two years later.

Alex Duncan

Above: Two Italian Line passenger-cargo ships, the *Sebastiano Caboto* and the *Ugolino Vivaldi*, were chartered to Lloyd Triestino in 1949-51 for their Italy-Australia service. They were refitted to carry 100 cabin class and as many as 735 in third class. Several years later, another Italian Line ship, the *Paolo Toscanelli*, was chartered to Lloyd Triestino for five trips out to Australia.

Below: In the early1950s, Lloyd Triestino built three sets of sisterships to replace their wartime losses. The first three - the *Australia, Neptunia* and *Oceania* (shown at Cape Town) - were built at Trieste in 1951. At 13,100 tons, they carried passengers in three classes: 280 in first, 120 in second and 392 in third. They sailed mostly at monthly intervals from Genoa, Naples and Messina to Port Said, Suez, Aden, Colombo, Djakarta, Fremantle, Melbourne and Sydney. In 1963, they were transferred to the Italian Line, becoming the popular 'Three Musicians' for South American service.   *Both, Alex Duncan*

Above: The next Lloyd Triestino set, while similar to the *Australia* class, were some 2,000 tons smaller and carried fewer passengers (148 in first class, 298 in tourist). Named *Africa* (shown) and *Europa,* they were commissioned in 1952. This pair was assigned to the African trades - departing from Trieste, Venice and Brindisi for Port Said, Suez, Aden, Mogadishu, Mombasa, Dar-es-Salaam, Beira, Durban, Cape Town and finally Port Elizabeth.   *Sal Scannella collection*

Right: The *Africa* and *Europa* finished their Lloyd Triestino sailings in 1976. The *Africa* was kept in reserve by her owners, but as the *Protea* (shown at Trieste and under Panamanian colors) and presumably with the intention of converting her for cruising. This never came to pass. Instead, she was sold to Taiwanese shipbreakers in March 1980 and scrapped at Kaohsiung. The *Europa* was sold to Arabian interests, who renamed her as the *Blue Sea* for Moslem pilgrim service. It was, however, a very short-lived new career. On November 12th 1976, while in Djeddah harbor, she caught fire and then sank at her moorings.   *Antonio Scrimali*

Later, Captain Calvillo was sent to one of Lloyd Triestino's largest liners, the 27,000-ton *Galileo Galilei* (today Celebrity Cruises' *Meridian* while her former twin sister, the *Guglielmo Marconi*, is now the *Costa Riviera* of the Costa Line) when she sailed the Italy-Australia run. "We carried many, many Italian and Greek immigrants to new lives in Australia, but then, by the 1970s, we began to have fewer and fewer passengers. And so, in 1979-81, we went cruising only - to Scandinavia, around the Mediterranean and into the Black Sea - for ICI, Italian Cruises International. In

the end, we were chartered to Chandris Cruises and carried a special Greek supervisor aboard. But in winters, we were laid-up at Genoa. Thirty-five crew and myself looked after the quiet *Galileo.* We did light maintenance mostly on that otherwise empty ship."

Captain Calvillo had just passed his 46th year at sea by the time we met aboard a Caribbean cruise on Carnival's *Festivale.* He had joined Carnival in 1986. A wonderfully gracious man, he concluded our visit with the words, "I'm sentimental for those great days of the old ocean liners. It was a golden era! "

Above: Lloyd Triestino added another pair to their fleet in 1953, the *Asia* and the *Victoria*. At 11,700 tons they looked quite similar to the earlier ships, but had their berthing arranged in reverse numbers - 290 in first class and 141 in tourist. They sailed every month from Genoa and Naples to Port Said, Suez, Aden, Karachi, Bombay, Djakarta, Singapore, Hong Kong, Manila and back to Naples and Genoa via Singapore, Bombay, Karachi and Suez. Naples to Bombay took 12 days, to Singapore 23 days and to Hong Kong 27 days. In the early 1960s, first class fares to Hong Kong started at $605; tourist class rates began at $425.

V.H. Young & L. A. Sawyer

Below: There were plans in the early 1970s, initiated by the Finmare Group, to convert some of these Lloyd Triestino passenger ships for Mediterranean cruising. This never materialized, however. The *Victoria* was withdrawn in late summer 1974, but then found further service with another Finmare member, the Adriatica Line. Mostly, she was used in local services from Italian ports to Egypt and Lebanon and on occasional cruises. She remained in this service until laid-up in June 1977. A year or so later, she was sold to the Youth-With-A-Mission Organisation. Renamed *Anastasis* , she has been a roving, worldwide floating missionary ship ever since. In 1982, she was re-registered at Malta and, in 1986, underwent an extensive refit at Victoria, British Columbia. She served Central America and Mexico in 1988 and then visted the US East Coast and Northern Europe in 1993-94.

Steffen Weirauch

Right: The *Asia* was retired by the Italians and laid-up at Trieste in April 1975. Shortly thereafter, she was sold to Lebanese buyers and rebuilt as the livestock carrier *Persia*. She changed hands again, in 1984, going to different Lebanese interests and becoming the *Norleb*. She finally ended her days, in December 1985, when she was handed over to shipbreaking crews at Gadani Beach in Pakistan. *Steffen Weirauch*

Below: In the 1960s, Italian shipyards produced some of the finest and most notable passenger liners of the day. There were the *Michelangelo* and the *Raffaello*, the *Oceanic* and the *Eugenio C.* There were also two large and fast Lloyd Triestino liners. Coming from the ever-busy Cantieri Riuniti dell 'Adriatico yards, the *Galileo Galilei* was delivered in April 1963; her identical sister, the *Guglielmo Marconi* (shown), in the following November. At 27,900 tons and 702 feet in length, they had modern acommodations for as many as 1,700 passengers - 100 in first class, 200 interchangeable and 1,400 in tourist. Designed with some basic similiarities to the trans-Atlantic *Leonardo Da Vinci*, capable of a top speed of 27.5 knots and with such press-worthy novelties as telescopic funnel tops, they also brought greatly improved standards to the predominantly low-fare Australian migrant trade. Replacing the earlier *Australia* class, these new ships could make the passage from Genoa all the way to Sydney via Suez in just over three weeks. "They were big, very nice and very fast steamers", recalled Captain Claudio Ciappina, who served aboard both sisters as a cadet and who later became master of the Italian-built cruiseship *Renaissance Three.* "Undoubtedly, they were the fastest and finest Italian liners ever to sail on the Australian route". *Roger Sherlock*

Above: These newest of Lloyd Triestino liners became, in fact, their last passenger ships. In their final years, in the 1970s, they often returned home from Australia and New Zealand via Panama and the Caribbean, a last ditch effort to secure more passengers. In 1976, the *Marconi* was loaned for a short time to the Italian Line to run East Coast of South America sailings together with the *Cristoforo Colombo*. This ended when she was laid-up at Naples in June 1977. Thereafter, both ships did some cruising - the *Galileo* was chartered to Chandris Cruises for European service while the *Marconi* attempted to revive Italian Line's cruise service out of New York. She is shown arriving on her inaugural call there in December 1978.   *Italian Line Cruises International*

Left: These voyages were complicated by financial as well as staffing problems. Furthermore, in order to be properly competitive, both ships needed long, expensive modernisations. Their roots in the Australian migrant trade showed. Even their Italian cooking and service failed to win many praises. The Italian Government, prodded by powerful, job-hungry maritime unions, hoped to see the ships remain in service. In the end, they spent more time laid-up near Genoa Airport than actually sailing. In November 1983, both of them were sold - the *Galileo Galilei* to Chandris-Fantasy Cruises, who refitted her as the Panamanian-registered *Galileo* and then later, in 1989-90, as the extensively rebuilt *Meridian;* and the *Marconi* to the Costa Line, for complete rebuilding as the *Costa Riviera.*   *Steffen Weirauch*

Chapter Three
Adriatica Line

Another member of the Italian Government's Finmare Group is the Venice-based Adriatica Line (Adriatica SpA di Navigazione). Their interests are in the Eastern Mediterranean and continue to this day with passenger ferries as well as cargo vessels. But like the Italian Line and Lloyd Triestino, they too were devastated by the Second World War. Most of their 42-ship pre-War fleet was lost by 1945.

Their lone survivor of any size was the 9,314-ton *Esperia*, laid down in 1941, but not completed until 1949. First intended to be called *Ausonia*, she was finished by Cantieri Riuniti dell'Adriatico at Monfalcone as *Esperia*. She remained the Adriatica Line's flagship until 1957, when the new and larger *Ausonia* came into service.

The 19-knot *Esperia* was used for all of her life on Adriatica's Express run between Italy, Egypt and Lebanon. The 11-day round voyages were routed between Genoa, Naples, Alexandria and Beirut returning via Piraeus, Syracuse, Naples and Marseilles. A weekly service was maintained in conjunction with the *Ausonia* which sailed from Trieste, Venice and Brindisi. Partially air-conditioned, the *Esperia* carried 472 passengers plus considerable freight in four holds. There were 151 berths in first class, 81 in second class and 240 in tourist (ranging from 8-berth cabins to 16-bunk dormitories). After sailing for nearly 25 years, the *Esperia* went to the scrappers in 1973.

Alex Duncan

Below: The Italian Government was very keen about rebuilding its post-war passenger ship fleet and so, following the completion of the *Esperia* , the Adriatica Line was promised no less than seven new passenger-cargo ships. The 5,173 *Enotria* (shown sailing from Naples) was the first and was launched at Ansaldo's Livorno yard in 1950. A twin sister, the *Messapia*, arrived two years later. Smart-looking little motorliners, they carried three classes of passengers: 76 in first, 44 in second and 162 in third. They were routed on 11-day round voyages, alternating between the east and west coasts of Italy: Either Genoa and Naples or Trieste, Venice and Brindisi to Limassol, Haifa, Larnaca, Piraeus and then back to Italy. Both the *Enotria* and the *Messapia* were sold, in July 1975, to Saudi Arabia's Orri Navigation Company for use in the Moslem pilgrim trades. The *Enotria* became the *Kawther* before being lost in 1980 when, during a storm, she was driven against a breakwater at Piraeus, Greece and badly damaged. She was scrapped a year later at nearby Elefsina. The *Messapia*, which became the *Zamzam*, sailed until 1980 as well. She was then laid-up at Port Suez and probably remains there to this day.

Alex Duncan

Above: Smaller versions of the *Enotria* and the *Messapia*, the 4,755-ton sisters *San Giorgio* and *San Marco* were added to the Adriatica fleet in 1956. They were built by Cantieri Riuniti dell 'Adriatico for the 'fast service' to Greece and Turkey. Typical of this line's ships, they alternated their sailings: Genoa and Naples or Trieste, Venice and Bari to Piraeus, Istanbul, Izmir and then home via Piraeus. The Genoa ship also called at Marseilles. Otherwise, the *San Marco* was notable in being the first Italian passenger ship to be fitted with fin stablizers. Despite their rather small size, these ships carried classes as well - 92 in a very pleasant air-conditioned first class; 45 in second class, which was also air-conditioned and finally 66 in tourist class, which was rather spartan and lacked air-conditioning. In the late 1960s, the berthing on these ships was revised to 92 first class and 102 tourist class. Like many Italian passenger ships of the post-war years, the *San Giorgio* and *San Marco* had sleek, contemporary decor which is said to have given them an air of spaciousness.   *Roger Sherlock*

Below: After twenty years on the Eastern Mediterranean run, the *San Giorgio* was sold, in August 1976, to become the *City of Andros* for Greece's Cycladic Cruises. In 1984, she was thoroughly rebuilt as the cruiseship *Ocean Islander* for Ocean Cruise Lines (shown sailing with the larger *Ocean Princess*, the former *Italia* of Costa). She flew the Bahamian flag and divided her time mostly between the Mediterranean in summers and the Caribbean in wintertime. She was sold again, in 1990, to the Royal Safari Club Ltd. for East African and Indian Ocean cruising as the *Royal Star*. The *San Marco* which had finished her Adriatica schedules in December 1975 was eventually also sold to Cycladic Cruises and was rebuilt as their cruiseship *City of Myconos*. After cruising Aegean waters for some years, she was laid-up as we went to press.   *Ocean Cruise Lines*

Above: Unquestionably, Adriatica Line's flagship, the 522-foot long *Ausonia*, was one of Italy's finest liners of the 1950s. She followed the splendid design of the *Andrea Doria*. Launched in August 1956, she entered service in October 1957. She was marketed at the time as the 'largest and fastest liner operating solely in the Mediterranean'. While having a service speed of 20 knots, she reached well over 23 knots during her sea trials. Fully air-conditioned, the 11,879-ton *Ausonia* had highly praised accommodations, once again done in very contemporary Italian styles, for 529 passengers - divided as 181 in first class, 118 in second and 230 third. She was also certified for 70 deck passengers. When she was withdrawn in September 1977, it was the end of Adriatica's conventional passenger ship services. Finmare took over the *Ausonia* and thereafter placed her on charter to Italian Line Cruises International and then, in 1982, to the Grimaldi-Siosa Group, for whom she still operates as a very successful Mediterranean cruiseship.   *Michael D. J. Lennon*

Right: Adriatica added three identical sisters in 1959 - the *Bernina* (shown at Naples), the *Brennero* and the *Stelvio*. Designed to provide weekly sailings from Italian ports, they worked a 19-day schedule to the Eastern Mediterranean. Alternating from Marseilles, Genoa, Naples Livorno and Catania or Trieste, Venice and Bari, they sailed to Alexandria, Port Said, Beirut, Famagusta, Latakia, Iskenderun, Mersin, Limassol, Rhodes, Izmir, Candia and finally Piraeus on the return. At 4,400 tons , they had considerable freight space (in five holds) and carried just 81 all-first class passengers. About a third of their cabins had private bathrooms. They were fully air-conditioned, stabilized and had outdoor swimming pools.   *Alex Duncan*

Left: These three ships continued in Adriatica service until the winter of 1976, when they were sold. The *Bernina* and the *Brennero* went to Egyptian buyers called Arab Navigators. Renamed *Abu El Kassem* and *El Hassam* (shown at Alexandria), they were intended for Moslem pilgrim services, but failed to obtain proper certification. They were laid-up in the outer waters of Alexandria harbor. Years later, in 1983, and after considerable neglect, I saw them from the top deck of the inbound *Eugenio C.* Then, a few years later, in 1989, I saw them once again, but from the arriving *Achille Lauro.* By then, however, one was lying half-sunk; the other had a severe list. Clearly they could be of no further interest except to the scrappers.

Steffen Weirauch

Right: The *Stelvio* was sold to the Greek-flag Cycladic Cruises and was to become the cruiseship *City of Rhodes*, but remained laid-up in the backwaters near Piraeus. In 1984, it was rumored that she would be rebuilt by Ocean Cruise Lines and become their *Ocean Ambassador.* But this project never developed and the ex-*Stelvio* remained at her moorings. With little hope, she was finally scrapped at Eleusis in 1986. Steffen Weirauch

Left: Adriatica's last newly-built conventional passenger ship was something unusual to the fleet. The 3,763-ton *Illiria*, built at Naples in 1962, was primarily a little cruiseship. She was designed to sail about two-thirds of the year on 13-day Mediterranean cruises from Trieste, Venice and Ancona. The 333-foot long ship had space for 181 all-first class passengers. She was finally sold, in 1975, to Greek buyers, the Blue Aegean Sea Line and later to other Greeks called Classical Cruises. Her itineraries were quite diverse: the Mediterranean and Black Seas, the Norwegian fjords, Spitsbergen, the Canadian Maritimes, the Amazon, Antarctica, the Far East and Southeast Asia. In 1994, she was sold to P&O Spice Island Cruises and, as the *Bali Sea Dancer*, makes three and four-day cruises from Bali to Lombok and Komodo. In this photograph, the former *Illiria* is shown at Copenhagen on August 24th 1989. The *Dawn Princess*, the former *Fairwind* of Sitmar Cruises, is just ahead of her. Ove Nielsen

Chapter Four
Costa Line

The Costa Line was for a time, in the early 1980s, the largest cruise company in the Western World. Only the Soviet fleet was larger. At its peak, Costa operated ten passenger ships. Started as an edible oil concern in 1860 and then spread into shipping in 1924, the company ran only cargo ships until February 1947 when their freighter *Maria C.* left Genoa for South America carrying passengers in temporary accommodation. But Costa passenger service really began in March 1948, the date of the first sailing of the *Anna C.*, a 12,000-tonner that had been the *Southern Prince* of the Furness Withy's Prince Line. Rebuilt for Latin American migrant service, she quickly developed a strong reputation for her overall comfort, shipboard style and her kitchens. Furthermore, the *Anna C.* was distinctive: she was Italy's first air-conditioned passenger ship. Later used as a cruiseship, she finished her days at La Spezia in December 1971.

A neatly dressed-overall *Anna C.*

V. H. Young & L. A. Sawyer

Right: Yet another Italian post-war conversion from freighter to passenger ship, the 8,604-ton *Andrea C.* was originally built at Richmond, California as the standardized cargo ship *Ocean Virtue* in 1942. She was sold to Costa in 1947 and soon thereafter re-engined and rebuilt for the Genoa-South America run.

Schiffsfotos Jansen

Left: Beginning in the 1960s, the 442-foot long *Andrea C.* did considerable cruising - the Mediterranean, the Caribbean and along the South American coast. In her final years, she cruised in the summers from Venice. She is shown being demolished at La Spezia in 1982.

Antonio Scrimali

Below: The 1914-built American coastal cargo ship *Medina* was rebuilt after the Second World War as the passenger ship *Roma* and then, after 1952, sailed for Costa as the *Franca C.* on the Central American run. *Everett Viez collection*

Left: In 1959, surpassed by larger tonnage and already 45 years old, the 6,549-ton *Franca C.* was rebuilt as an all-first class cruiseship. With 367 maximum berths, she cruised the Mediterranean in summers, but in winter became one of the very first ships to use Port Everglades, Florida as a base. Later, in 1968, while sailing from San Juan, Puerto Rico, she offered the very first air-sea combination cruises in the then infant US cruise industry. In 1977, she was sold by Costa and became the West German-owned, Maltese-registered missionary ship and floating book fair *Doulos*. She remains in this service and has been refitted so as to last until 2014, her 100th birthday!

Everett Viez collection

Within ten years of that first passenger sailing aboard the rebuilt *Anna C.*, the Costa Line introduced their first brand new liner. This Costa flagship was something of a 'cousin' to the Italian Line's *Andrea Doria* and *Cristoforo Colombo*. Launched from the same Ansaldo shipyards at Genoa in March 1957, she was named *Federico C*. At 20,400 tons and with a capacity for 1,279 passengers in three classes, she was almost immediately acclaimed as one of the finest ships of her day. She was certainly the most stunning on the South American run. Twenty-five years later, in 1983, she was sold to Premier Cruise Lines and, as the *Starship Royale*, sailed on short cruises between Florida and the Bahamas. In 1989, she hoisted the colors of the Greek-owned Dolphin Cruise Line and was renamed *Sea Breeze 1* for 7-day Miami-Caribbean service. She remains with Dolphin at the time of writing.

Antonio Scrimali

The handsome-looking *Bianca C.* leaving Genoa on her maiden voyage for Costa, April 4th 1959.

Maurizio Eliseo collection

Sad Ending for the Bianca C.

In the horse-shoe shaped inner harbor of St George's on the Caribbean island of Grenada, a prominent and imposing statue stands along the waterfront embankment. It is "Christ of the Deep". With the arms and head facing upwards, it is a symbol of hope and reassurance, but also, perhaps most of all, of gratitude. It was presented to the local people by the Costa family. It was given in thanks for the enormous help rendered by the Grenadians when the liner *Bianca C.* burned and then sank in October 1961. Now well over thirty years ago, the ship's remains are still in a watery grave outside the harbor entrance.

The 594-foot long motorship was just about to sail with a full load of West Indian migrants bound for European resettlement when a tank burst and started an engine room fire. "The blaze spread quickly," according to Captain D. Julian Rapier, a Grenada harbor pilot. "The ship was still at her anchorage. It was a Sunday morning. Onboard, there was an immediate call to abandon ship. The Italian crew had to man a huge effort just to prevent the panicky passengers from returning to their cabins to collect their belongings. All of the generators had shut down and so there was great difficulty in launching the lifeboats. Some boats were finally lowered, but the crew also put cargo nets along the sides and the passengers slid down these."

"Ashore, people saw the huge clouds of smoke. The *Bianca C.* burned for two days. At night, the steel plates were glowing red. It was like something out of a forge. Finally, she was put under tow by a British warship, the HMS *Londonderry*, and was to be deliberately run aground. But this failed. The lines were cut and they just let her sink."

"Quite amazingly, there were only four casualties. One crewman was blown to bits in the explosion and another was so badly burned that he died in the lifeboat. Two others died in a Maracaibo hospital about two weeks later."

"In Grenada, we did not have enough hotels for the survivors," according to Captain Rapier.

"Grenadians each took two and three passengers into their homes, some for as long as two or three weeks. The very grateful Costa Line later sent the statue as a way of thanks. First located in our harbor entrance, it was moved to the safer inner basin in 1988 and now rests on the pillars and foundations from two, old local churches."

The 17,300-ton *Bianca C.* had a comparatively brief career. Laid down in 1939, she was intended to be the new queen of the French colonial run from Marseilles out to Indo-China. Named *Marechal Petain* and then *La Marseillaise*, the War interrupted her delivery for a full ten years, until 1949. But decolonization would spell a rather hasty end to her service East of Suez and so, by 1957, she was plying the North Atlantic as the Swiss-owned *Arosa Sky* for the shortlived Arosa Line. Less than two years later, she changed owners again, this time hoisting the Costa Line houseflag. Upgraded and modernized, she was among the nicest tourist class/migrant ships of her time. Her decor, for example, was done in fine Mediterranean contemporary and her particularly spacious outer decks included two tiled pools and umbrella-lined lidos. She carried 202 in first class and 1,030 in tourist. She was routed from Naples, Genoa, Cannes, Barcelona, Madeira and Tenerife to La Guaira and such Caribbean islands as Barbados, Grenada, St Vincent and Martinique. As the *Bianca C.*, she also ran some winter cruises in 1959-61 from New York and then Port Everglades. Under charter to Simmons Cruises, some sample New York cruises in early 1960 included nine days to Port-au-Prince and Kingston, from $220; and sixteen days to San Juan, St Thomas, Martinique, La Guaira, Curacao, Kingston, Port-au-Prince and Nassau, from $435.

Her remains are still an attraction to more experienced divers. But rather expectedly, she is hardly the same ship. "Her masts were detonated at deck level," reported Captain Rapier, "and both her propellers are off. The bridge melted in the fire and now even the funnel is gone. It was all a great tragedy."

"It was a very unusual arrangement. The *Melanesien* was owned by Costa, operated by the Cogedar Line and chartered to Messageries Maritimes, the big French shipping line based at Marseilles", noted Captain Elvio Arimondo. "She sailed on 4-month round voyages from Marseilles over to Algeria, then across to the Caribbean and Panama and down to Tahiti and French New Guinea and Australia. She carried mostly French Government passengers, mail and lots of general cargo. There were two nationalities in her crew - French in the hotel department and Italians in deck and engine". She had been built in 1926 as Rotterdam Lloyd's *Indrapoera*. They sold her to Genoese owners in 1956 and she was briefly renamed *Assuncion*. Costa bought her in 1957 and called her *Bianca C.* but when she started running for Messageries Maritimes she became *Melanesien*. She had berthing for 180 passengers - 100 in first class, 80 in third and was scrapped in 1963.

World Ship Society

The French liner *Provence*, used on the Marseilles-South Amercan run, was sold to Costa in 1965 and renamed *Enrico C.* (changed to *Enrico Costa* in 1983). For a time, she continued in South American service, partnered with the *Andrea C.*, the *Federico C.* and the brand new *Eugenio C.* Beginning in the 1970s, she was used mostly for cruising and was extensively refitted in 1989. She was sold, however, to Starlauro in September 1994 and renamed *Symphony.*

Steffen Weirauch

If the *Federico C.* of 1958 was acclaimed as the finest Italian liner on the South America run when she was built, Costa's magnificent *Eugenio C.* of 1966 was unquestionably the very finest liner of any flag in that southern service. Ordered in 1962 and then launched in November 1964, she was built by Cantieri Riuniti dell'Adriatico at their Monfalcone yard. That same company was then quite busy - they were adding the finishing touches to Italian Line's *Raffaello* and to Home Lines' *Oceanic*. With an exceptional trial speed of 27 knots, the 712-foot long *Eugenio C.* was also the very fastest liner in South American service. She was routed, after her maiden sailing in August 1966, between Genoa, Cannes, Lisbon, Rio de Janeiro, Santos, Montevideo and Buenos Aires. She continued with the then customary three-class arrangement for her passengers: 186 in first class, 350 in cabin and 1,100 in tourist. Used for fulltime cruising in later years and renamed *Eugenio Costa* in 1987, she was to have been transferred to the shortlived American Family Cruises and become the *American Adveture.* This did not come to pass and instead, in 1994, she was refitted for further Costa service. In fact, she has been sold to the Bremer-Vulkan shipyard in part-payment for a new ship they are building for Costa, but has been immediately chartered back for further Costa cruising.   *Costa Line*

Costa bought the French Line's *Flandre* in 1968. Launched in October 1951, she had been used on the Le Havre-New York and later the Le Havre-West Indies routes. Costa rebuilt her as the cruiseship *Carla C.* and she went into immediate charter work. She sailed on American West Coast cruises - to the Mexican Riviera mostly and later on trans-Panama trips - for a young company called Princess Cruises. She was in fact marketed as the *Princess Carla,* but never renamed officially. On these voyages, she provided the inspirational setting for the novel and later the television series, "The Love Boat". In 1970, she went into Costa's own service, sailing mostly in Caribbean waters out of San Juan. In 1974-75, she underwent major surgery in Holland, changing from a steamship to a motorliner. She was sold to Epirotiki Lines in 1992 and became their *Pallas Athena.* Sadly, however, she was seriously damaged by fire (as shown outside Piraeus harbor) on March 24th 1994 and was eventually delivered to Turkish breakers.

Princess Cruises (above); Antonio Scrimali (below)

Above: In late 1967, Norwegian America Line's handsome 577-foot long *Oslofjord* (built 1949) began a charter to the Greek Line for cruises out of Southampton. But a year later she was chartered to Costa and became the *Fulvia*. She took on an Italian hotel staff but retained her Norwegian officers and sailed the Mediterranean in summer, the Caribbean in winter. She met a premature end while on a summer cruise to the Canary Islands. On July 20th 1970, she caught fire off Tenerife and burned ferociously, with her upper decks melting and the funnel collapsing within. She had to be abandoned and later the burnt-out hulk was allowed to sink. *J. K. Byass*

Below: After having been the Cunard passenger-cargo liner *Media* (built 1947 for the Liverpool-New York run) and then extensively rebuilt for Cogedar Line's Australian migrant service as the *Flavia* (in 1962), the same ship began sailing for Costa in 1968. She ran Florida-Bahamas cruises mostly, until sold to Hong Kong interests in 1982. *Costa Line*

Right: Having left the Costa fleet, she met a sad end. Renamed *Flavian*, then *Lavian* and finally *Lavia*, she was being refitted for further cruise service when, on January 7th 1989, she caught fire in Hong Kong harbor and later capsized. Beyond economic repair, she was delivered to Taiwanese scrappers that summer. *South China Morning Post*

Below: The 12,219-ton, 476-passenger *Italia*, built in 1967, had a troubled early career before being chartered by Costa from an Italian bank in 1973. Costa bought her outright four years later and used her exclusively for cruising. She is shown arriving at Valletta, Malta on September 11th 1978.

Michael Cassar

Below: Sold to Ocean Cruise Lines in 1983 and renamed *Ocean Princess*, she cruised to South America, the Caribbean and northern Europe. She is shown at Copenhagen in August 1989 along with the *Mermoz*, the *Crown Odyssey* and (barely visible) the *Istra*. She ran aground, however, during an Amazon River cruise on March 1st 1993 and was badly damaged. Flooding occurred to two passenger decks and the engine room. Later repaired and renamed *Sea Prince*, she was to resume cruising in Spring 1995 for the Greek-owned Sunshine Cruise Lines but had a fire on May 26th. She was then sold to Louis Cruise Lines and has become the *Princess Oceania* for Eastern Mediterranean service. *Ove Nielsen*

Left: Two superb British cargo liners, the 12-passenger *Port of Sydney* and *Port of Melbourne* (shown) of the Port Line, were sold to the Greek-flag Carras Group in 1972 and later rebuilt as the cruiseships *Daphne* and *Danae* respectively. Extremely luxurious, they were restyled to carry less than 500 passengers each. They were used on worldwide itineraries, but this Carras venture was unfortunately not a great financial success.   *Schiffsfotos Jansen*

In 1979, the *Daphne* and the *Danae* (shown) were leased to Costa and then bought outright in 1985. They were officially transferred to a Panamanian-flag holding company, the Independent Continental Lines and gained a very good reputation. During a pre-World Cruise refit in December 1991, the *Danae* was badly damaged by a fire while at a Genoa shipyard. At first declared a complete loss, she was sold to Greek buyers, towed to Greece as the *Anar* and later renamed the *Starlight Express*. After lengthy repairs, she resumed cruising in 1994, but as the *Baltica* on a German charter. The *Daphne,* which had been transferred to a Costa Cruises-Russian co-operative called Prestige Cruises, remains in service.

Costa Cruises

Right: Swedish American Line's *Kungsholm* of 1953 was considered one of the most charming trans-Atlantic and cruise liners of her time. She was sold to North German Lloyd in 1965 and sailed as their *Europa* until she joined Costa in late 1981. She was in fact sold to a Curacao-based holding company called Milestone, which was a division of the Costa Group. Intended to run some West German charter cruises, she was renamed *Columbus C.*, a reminder of the famed North German Lloyd *Columbus* of the 1920s and 30s. Early in 1984, however, with Costa trimming its fleet, there was a rumor that the 21,141-ton ship would be sold to the Chinese, who planned to run her as the *Friendship*. But charter work kept her in European waters.

Antonio Scrimali

It was on one of the charter voyages, on July 29th 1984, that she rammed the outer breakwater at Cadiz in Spain. Damaged, she continued to her berth but then developed a severe list. She was righted, only to sink upright at her pier. That November, she was pumped out and sold to scrappers at Barcelona. Demolition commenced on June 1st 1985. In this photograph, taken during the summer of 1984, the *Columbus C.* is half-sunk at Cadiz. Herself the former *Kungsholm* of 1953, she is stern-to-stern with P&O's *Sea Princess*, another ex-*Kungsholm*, but of 1966.

Author's photograph

Two Conversions

In 1986-87, Greece's Regency Cruises bought two out-of-work containerships with quite ambitious plans to rebuild them as cruiseships. These plans went astray and both ships eventually found their way into the Costa fleet.

The 16,000-ton containerships *Axel Johnson* and *Annie Johnson* had been built at Finland's Wartsila shipyards in 1969-70 for the Johnson Line. Rather quickly, they became unprofitable in an age of ever-larger, ever-more efficient mega-containerships. They were eventually laid-up and then offered for sale. Bought by companies associated with Regency Cruises, the *Axel Johnson* became the *Regent Moon* under the Cypriot flag, while the *Annie Johnson* became the *Regent Sky*. They were taken to Eleusis Bay, near Piraeus, for conversion. Unfortunately, little else happened and they sat at their anchorages facing at least an extended wait. Clearly, Regency had some second thoughts, especially after they added the former *Rhapsody* (*Regent Star*) and then the ex-*Royal Odyssey* (*Regent Sun*) to their fleet. Then, in 1986, the intended *Regent Moon* (ex-*Axel Johnson*) was moved to Genoa, supposedly to be converted as the *Sea Venture*. This never materialized and later, in 1988, she was reportedly sold to Navyclub, a Naples-based cruise and tour firm. She was renamed *Italia* and, once again, there were reports that she would be rebuilt. Finally, in the fall of 1988, she was sold to Costa, who were then wanting to replace their ageing *Enrico Costa*. She was thoroughly rebuilt, emerging as the 25,441-ton, 1,025-passenger *Costa Marina* in the late summer of 1990. Her sister, the intended *Regent Sky* (ex-*Annie Johnson*) was at one time reported to have been sold to Turkish scrappers but she remained at her Greek moorings. There were further reports that she was to be rebuilt as a Mediterranean ferry, but finally, in the summer of 1990, she too was sold to Costa. The Genoa directors were obviously pleased with the conversion results of the *Costa Marina*. Renamed *Costa Allegra* (*Costa Azzura* had been the initial choice), she was rebuilt as well, at the famed Mariotti shipyards, a firm long experienced with passenger ship conversions and refits. Two years later, in December 1992, she entered Costa's winter Caribbean service (in summer, she made seven thirteen-day Western Mediterranean and Northern European cruises).

Left: The unusual stern-section and funnel arrangement of the *Costa Marina* is very evident in this photograph taken at Lisbon. *Luis Miguel Correia*

Right: The *Costa Allegra* being fitted-out at Genoa's Mariotti shipyards.

Centre: Dressed in flags and with her funnels not yet fully painted in Costa colors, the *Costa Allegra* prepares to depart on her sea trials.

Both, Paolo Piccione collection

The interiors of the *Costa Allegra* are fine examples of modern Italian style.   *Costa Cruises*

In 1989, Costa Cruises embarked on a $1 billion renewal program. Certainly their most ambitious project yet, it included the conversion of the two ex-Swedish containerships and, with the Italian Government's generous financial assistance, the building of two 53,000-ton liners. Costing $325 million each and therefore advertised as the 'most expensive cruiseships ever built', these 1,300-passenger sisters were constructed by the Fincantieri yard at Marghera near Venice. The *Costa Classica* was completed in late 1991; the *Costa Romantica* arrived in the fall of 1993. The *Romantica* is shown left while still under construction.

Paolo Piccione collection
The *Romantica* is also shown below, later, during a call at Lisbon.

Luis Miguel Correia

COSTA CLASSICA and COSTA ROMANTICA

The design and the decor of both the *Costa Classica* and *Costa Romantica* are of a very modern Italian style. The *Classica* (shown in these two interior views) is, in fact, the more radical of the two, perhaps the more severe. Some critics have compared her interiors to a very contemporary museum. Alternately, the *Romantica* leans more to the subdued, more to traditional Italian style. To some, the departure might seem too radical - perhaps too much marble in some areas, too ornate in others and some fixtures are too modern in design. However, such earlier liners as the *Andrea Doria*, the *Leonardo Da Vinci* and the *Michelangelo* were once looked upon in the same way because of their extreme modern Italian styles.

Differences between these new Costa sisters include more suites on board the *Costa Romantica*. These take the place of the outdoor spa area on the *Classica*. On the *Romantica* , the spa has been reduced in size and moved elsewhere. The general staterooms differ as well. On board the *Romantica,* cabin furniture has a different layout that actually makes these rooms seem larger. But in almost all other ways, the ships are quite comparable. Both divide their time between winters in the Caribbean and the remainder in European waters, which includes not only Mediterranean cruising from Genoa and Venice, but Scandinavian itineraries from Amsterdam.

The success of this pair along with Costa's desire to dominate the European cruise market in particular led to designs for a even larger pair: 75,000-ton sisters originally to be called *Costa Lirica* and *Costa Magica*. But instead of being built at Fincantieri in Italty, the contract for the first of these 2,274-passenger ships went to Germany's Bremer-Vulkan yard at Bremen. She was

laid down in November 1994, but as the *Costa Victoria*. A second, near sister, larger still at 78,000 tons, will be the *Costa Olimpia*, due in 1997.

Costa Cruises

55

Chapter Five

Sitmar

Early History

Sitmar, an abbreviation for Societa Italiana Trasporti Marittimi, was created by Alexandre Vlasov (and thus the "V" on the funnels for many years), a Russian, who fled from his native Odessa in 1917. Together with his son Boris, who in later years became chairman of Sitmar and its parent, the Monte Carlo-based V Group, he set up companies in Romania, Poland and Italy. The senior Vlasov had a keen, highly intuitive ability for ships and shipping. In the hard-pressed Depression years of the 1930s, he created his first fleet, which consisted mostly of "coal ships," which made great profits carrying that much needed mineral from Poland around continental Europe to Italy. This Vlasov cargo fleet expanded steadily when, just after the Second World War, both father and son saw equal potential in the passenger ship business, particularly in the migrant trades. And so, in 1947, the Vlasovs bought two surplus US Government "Victory Ships," the 7,600-ton *Vassar Victory*, which was renamed *Castelbianco*, and the *Wooster Victory*, which later became the *Castelverde*. (These names were amended slightly, to *Castel Bianco* and *Castel Verde*, in 1953). The simplest accommodations were installed at first for about 800 aboard each ship. However, even in these earliest days and considering their low-fare, often Government-sponsored clientele, they received praises for their Italian cooking and were said to be amongst the very best migrant ships then afloat. On their first voyages, most of their passengers were refugees and displaced persons, Europeans who were almost desperately seeking a new life elsewhere. Captain Franco Donnino served in these ships and recalled, "They were very functional ships, refitted for their special purpose. They were also notorious rollers. They even rolled in port! With their continuous rolling, it was always very difficult at sea. Almost everyone was sick - even the crew! Each ship had a few cabins and even fewer with private bathrooms. Mostly, there were large dormitories."

"Both ships were refitted further and improved in the early 1950s," added Captain Donnino. "In 1954, after sailing mostly from Genoa to Australia and occasionally to South America, we placed these two ships in Caribbean service, with migrants going from Genoa, Barcelona, Vigo, Corunna and Las Palmas to La Guaira in Venezuela. We then ran empty to Kingston, where we loaded Jamaican migrants, who were taken to Genoa and then placed on trains for resettlement in England. Occasionally, we would also take Venezuelans on these homeward trips. They were bound for holiday travel in Europe. By 1957, however, Sitmar wanted to progress to larger passenger ships and also wanted to strengthen its Australian services. These former freighters were simply too small. We sold them to the Spanish Line. The *Castel Bianco* became the *Begona* and the *Castel Verde* changed to *Montserrat*."

Quite popular in England-Spain-West Indies service

Above: The former Victory Class freighter *Vassar Victory* became one of Sitmar's first passenger ships, the *Castel Bianco,* which was used in austerity migrant service. *(Schiffsfotos Jansen) Below:* The *Fairsea*, bought by Sitmar in 1949, had been a World War Two 'baby flattop', the aircraft carrier *Charger.*   *Antonio Scrimali*

for well over a decade, both ships were plagued with mechanical problems in their final years. The *Montserrat* actually broke down in mid-Atlantic in August 1970. The *Begona* was nearby at the time and took on her sister's 660 passengers. Left adrift for four days, the *Montserrat* was later towed to port and repaired. She remained in service until sold for scrap in early 1973. The *Begona* broke down in the Atlantic as well, in October 1974. With over 1,000 onboard, she was adrift for several days. Eventually towed to Barbados, her age coupled with the cost of repairs spelled her end. Towed back to Spain, she was delivered to scrappers on Christmas Eve.

In 1949, Sitmar added another converted passenger ship, the 11,800-ton *Fairsea*. She had been built in 1941, at the Sun Shipbuilding Company yard at Chester, Pennsylvania, and was intended to be the combination passenger-cargo liner *Rio De La Plata* for Moore-McCormack Lines' New York-East Coast of South America service.

In 1952, with encouraging forecasts for its Australian business, Sitmar added the 12,100-ton *Castel Felice*, the 'happy castle'. She had been the pre-war *Kenya* of the British India Line. Under the Italian colors, she had space for as many as 1,540 passengers (596 in first class, 944 in tourist). 'She was a very solid old ship, an excellent 'sea boat',' according to Captain Donninio, 'and could make the passage between Southampton and Sydney via Suez in 34 days'. A great success, she survived until the fall of 1970 when she was scrapped on Taiwan.   *Schiffsfotos Jansen*

She and her sisters were unusual in being American ships fitted with diesels instead of the far more customary steam turbines. Her completion was cancelled and instead she was bought, under emergency Wartime conditions, by the US Navy and then redesigned as the escort aircraft carrier *Charger*. Soon after completion in March 1942, she was loaned to Britain as part of the Lend-Lease Program and thereafter was known as the HMS *Charger*. Unharmed in the ensuing years, she was returned to the Americans in 1946 and, without further use, was laid-up. While she was declared surplus and might have been scrapped, she was placed instead on the Government disposal list and was auctioned-off to Sitmar in 1949. Her new owners were in fact a Sitmar subsidiary, the Alvion Steamship Company of Panama.

Renamed *Fairsea*, she was first rebuilt at the Bethlehem Steel shipyards at Hoboken, New Jersey and later outfitted at Genoa. She had very austere quarters for as many as 1,800 (later reduced to 1,440) so-called tourist class passengers. Mostly, she was used on the Australian run, carrying refugees and migrants on the outbound sailings only. Within several years, however, by February 1952, Alexandre Vlasov saw potential in a full Australian passenger service and so decided to carry homeward passengers as well. George Greishaber, formerly with the International Refugee Organization in Europe, joined Sitmar at this time and

soon opened their Sydney office. "That first office was actually located in a basement barbershop on Margaret Street. I had a secretary and, between us, we did everything. Our local corporate name was Navcot Australia Proprietary Limited. While the *Fairsea* became one of the first post-War migrant ships to carry refugees to New Zealand as well as to Australia, she also became the first of her type to carry passengers on homeward sailings. The five-week trip from Sydney to Naples was priced from £90. On the first sailing we had 75 passengers or just enough to pay the tolls in the Suez Canal. Almost immediately, we began to solicit travel agents and soon increased our business to 200 passengers on the third homeward sailing. Within two years, the *Fairsea* and our other ships were nearly filled to capacity. We attracted budget tourists, the Australian backpacker market. It was all a very smart move started by Mr Vlasov."

The year 1958 was most important in Sitmar's early passenger history. Among others, George Greishaber's tasks and responsibilities increased considerably. "Sitmar was always very fortunate to receive various passenger contracts to take passengers out to Australia. The first was from the International Refugee Organization, but even more important, in 1958, was the Australian Government's £10 assisted passage scheme'. It was a long-range effort to increase the

The 12,400-ton *Fairsky*, with all-tourist class space for 1,461 passengers, joined Sitmar's Australian run in June 1958. Expectedly, she too was a converted ship, having been built in 1941 at San Francisco. She had been launched as the freighter *Steel Artisan* for the Isthmian Lines, but then was redesigned and completed as the 'baby flattop' USS *Barnes* for the US Navy. In fact she was lent to the Royal Navy as HMS *Attacker*. Decommissioned in 1946 and laid-up, she was sold to National Bulk Carriers for conversion to an oil tanker. But these plans were shelved and instead she was sold to Sitmar in 1950. Renamed *Castel Forte*, she was to have become a freighter, but instead remained laid-up for seven years, until 1957. She was rebuilt as a passenger ship at New York and then at Genoa. Used for cruising in later years, she grounded in Djakarta Bay in June 1977 and was sold to Chinese shipbreakers. But then she was resold to the Marcos family of the Philippines and refitted as the casino ship *Philippine Tourist*. Moored in Manila harbor, it was all shortlived, however, as she burnt out at her pier on November 3rd 1979. Her remains were later scrapped at Hong Kong.   *Roger Sherlock*

nation's population, particularly its industrial and technological forces. The Government paid the balance of all fares and provided us with solidly-booked ships for the next ten years (this contract remained until 1968, when it was given to the rival Chandris Lines). We had the *Fairsea* and then the *Castel Felice*, but we still needed a third passenger ship and so we added the *Fairsky* in June 1958. At the time, she was the first fully air-conditioned passenger ship on the Australian run. Our general routing for these three ships was from Southampton (and sometimes from Bremerhaven) to Port Said, Suez, Aden, Fremantle or Adelaide, Melbourne and then Sydney. Occasionally, the ships might continue to Auckland or Wellington as well. Homewards, they were routed via Singapore, Colombo, Aden, Suez, Port Said, Naples and then Southampton."

"Considering that the population of Australia was six million in 1940 and that it reached fifty million by 1986, there has been enormous migration over the years," added Mr Greishaber. "This peaked in the decade between the late 1950s and the late 1960s.

Sitmar made great profits at this time. Outbound, we were full-up on every trip and homewards reached 75% or better. Of course, life onboard was not always too comfortable. We had dormitories, some with as many as 200 berths each, on all of our ships. Very, very few cabins had private facilities. But these standards were appropriate at the time. Of course, they were later upgraded and improved according to demand and as the competition increased."

By 1968, however, Sitmar's fortunes in both the Australian and the around-the-world passenger trades (they began returning to Europe via the Panama Canal) started to change - and change dramatically. While there was an increasing trend toward aircraft, the loss of the very lucrative Australian Government migrant contract to Chandris was the decisive blow. The steady, highly profitable employment for four Sitmar passenger liners (the largest of all, the *Fairstar*, had joined the *Fairsea*, the *Castel Felice* and the *Fairsky*) began to fall in the red. The *Fairsea* was actually the first to be withdrawn and Captain Donnino was aboard what proved to be her final sailing. "On June 29, 1969, when sailing

'The 21,600-ton *Fairstar* ran for our last 'line voyage' to Australia in 1973', noted George Greishaber. 'Briefly, we used her for summer Mediterranean cruises from Southampton, but we found that there wasn't sufficient business in the UK at that time. The *Fairstar* was then sent to Australia for year-round Pacific cruising'. She had joined Sitmar in 1963, having been Bibby Line's peacetime troopship *Oxfordshire* (built in 1957). Rebuilt in Holland with space for 1,910 all-tourist class passengers, she first entered Sitmar's Australian service in May 1964. At the time, the homeward itineraries were often amended to Auckland, Papeete, Balboa, Cristobal, Curacao, Lisbon and then Southampton. The *Fairstar* was sold, along with Sitmar Cruises, to the P&O Group in 1988. She remains in Australian cruise service. *Everett Viez collection*

from Tahiti to Panama with 985 passengers onboard, we were immobilized by a severe engine room fire. We didn't even have emergency power for a day or two and so we just drifted in the Pacific. Little by little, however, power was restored. But we still couldn't flush most of the toilets. We also had to use water from the swimming pool for washing, but this had to be rationed. At first, we waited for a nearby tug, which was towing a Japanese ship, but which later proved to be no help whatsoever. The tug was defective and was unable to tow us. It too had broken down. Soon afterward, our captain committed suicide. It was an extreme situation: no power, no tug, no captain! As

staff captain, I had to assume command. Fortunately, the American freighter *Louise Lykes* was nearby and offered to tow us to Balboa. We accepted and, at eight knots, this took eleven days. Once at Panama, we were given to a tug and finally had all power working except the main propulsion. The weary passengers were taken ashore and then flown to Europe."

"Unfortunately, the *Fairsea* - while always a happy ship and very well known in Australia - was not worth repairing. A skeleton crew stayed with her as she was towed across the Atlantic later that summer. She was then scrapped at La Spezia in Italy."

The former Cunarder *Sylvania*, Sitmar's *Fairwind* arrives off Port Everglades, Florida for the first time in 1972.

Everett Viez collection

Two Ex-Cunarders

By the late 'sixties Sitmar's Australian service was left with only two viable passenger ships, the *Fairsky* and the *Fairstar*, and less than encouraging prospects. According to George Greishaber, "Boris Vlasov (who had by this time replaced his father as chairman) realized that the once booming passenger trade out to Australia was doomed. But in one final effort he attempted to regain the Australian Government migrant contract (from Chandris) by offering two converted ex-Cunarders, the *Fairland* and the *Fairwind*. They were the former trans-Atlantic liners *Carinthia* and *Sylvania* of 1956 and 1957 respectively. They would have been the finest ships of their type in the Australian migrant and around-the-world tourist trades, but - in the final analysis - the fares would not have been competitive. The plans were changed, the ships remained in lay-up at Southampton for a time and the intended *Fairland*, while a suitable name for a migrant ship, was changed to *Fairsea*. The next plan was to run these ships from the North American West Coast to Australia and New Zealand in competition with the established Matson and P&O liners. Sitmar mounted a huge marketing program for this projected service, but the response was so poor that everything had to be cancelled. Instead, the ships were assigned to North American cruising - first from San Francisco and Los Angeles, and later from Port Everglades as well.

Both of them were thoroughly rebuilt at Trieste and then were recommissioned in 1971-72. At first, however, this cruise service had its problems. There were great losses (estimated at $5 million). Sitmar was completely unknown in the United States. It took us some time to establish ourselves, to develop a widespread and positive reputation, but the results were eventually beyond expectations. Sitmar Cruises became one of the best known and most popular cruise firms in American service."

"They were fantastic conversions - quite plain ships but of great quality in overall construction," recalled Jan Loeff, a member of the Sitmar sales department at San Francisco in the 1970s. "They were well-built ships that rode very well. They also had wonderful open promenade decks. Onboard, Sitmar service was like the old Italian Line - extremely good cuisine and excellent service. The Italian officers and crew had a certain style, which had great appeal. All of these gave us great distinction. We also had the competitive edge: we offered the first free air links in the US cruise industry. We flew passengers free from California to Florida to join the *Fairwind* cruises. Royal Caribbean Cruise Lines soon followed us."

In 1988, just before Sitmar Cruises was sold to P&O, there was some rethinking on the company's overall image. Besides being repainted in new livery, the

Above: Sold to P&O for their Princess Cruises division, the former *Fairwind* is shown arriving at Lisbon during a western European cruise as the *Dawn Princess*.   *Luis Miguel Correia*

Below: In US cruising, the *Fairsea* and the *Fairwind* had achieved considerable success, such that by the early 1980s, a third ship was needed. Once again, Sitmar engineers looked to a suitable second-hand vessel. They found the 19,300-ton oil workers' accommodation ship *Al Hasa,* the former Portuguese liner *Principe Perfeito* of 1961. Sitmar bought her in 1980 and, as the renamed *Fairsky*, she was to be rebuilt for American cruising. But the plans never left the drawing boards and instead it was decided that a brand-new, larger ship would be a better investment. The *Fairsky* was renamed *Vera* and then later sold to Greek tanker billionaire John S. Latsis, who renamed her *Mariana IX* and despatched her to Saudi Arabia for further service to oil crews. As of 1993, she has been laid-up in Eleusis Bay in Greece.   *Antonio Scrimali*

Sitmar commissioned the 46,314-ton *Fairsky* in ceremonies at Los Angeles in May 1984. Not only the company's largest ship yet, she was further unique in Sitmar history in being the line's first brand-new passenger ship. French-built and considered a great success, she had amenities such as circular swimming pools and hot tubs, closed circuit television systems, shopping arcades and even pizza parlours and an ice cream shop. From its early days carrying refugees and migrants, travelling in large, often crowded dormitories on board converted freighters and ex-wartime aircraft carriers, Sitmar had progressed to the contemporary age of sleek, all-white, purposely-built cruiseships. Transferred to Princess Cruises in 1988 and becoming the *Sky Princess*, the 790-foot liner is shown at New York's Pier 88 in May 1989. The *Cunard Princess* is berthed just across the same pier.

Port Authority of New York & New Jersey

Fairwind was renamed *Sitmar Fairwind*. But within months, in September, there was the transfer to P&O-Princess - the *Fairsea* became the *Fair Princess*, the *Sitmar Fairwind* changed to *Dawn Princess*. By this time, their itineraries had expanded considerably - to Hawaii, Australia, the South Pacific, South America, Northern Europe, the Mediterranean and to New England and the Canadian Maritimes. But as Princess added more and more tonnage, namely the 1,990-passenger mega-liners *Crown Princess* and *Regal Princess*, ships like the older (and increasingly costly and mechanically troublesome) ex-Sitmar sisters fell out of step. There had been recurrent rumours within the US cruise industry that they would join P&O's Australian

service. Instead, in the spring of 1993, the *Dawn Princess* was sold back to a former owner, the Monte Carlo-based V Group. The V Group owned the original Sitmar Cruises and today manages other cruise ships (such as Regency Cruises' *Regent Sun*) as well as being the parent to the new, super-deluxe Silversea Cruises.

Renamed *Albatros*, the former *Dawn Princess* has gone on long-term charter to one of Germany's biggest cruise-tour operators, Phoenix Reisen. She currently runs Scandinavian and Mediterranean cruises as well as a long, annual trip around-the-world. In 1995, the *Fair Princess* too, was sold to Regency Cruises who have called her *Regent Isle*.

Chapter Six
Grimaldi-Siosa

"The Grimaldi brothers were nephews of Achille Lauro, the founder and owner of the Lauro Line", according to Ugo Frangini, a purser who served with the Grimaldi-Siosa Lines for over thirty years. "Their mother, Amelia Grimaldi, was the sister of Achille Lauro."

The Fratelli Grimaldi (ie Grimaldi Brothers) went into the passenger ship business in the late 1940s. Like other Italians, they saw great potential (and fortunes to be made) in the post-War migrant and refugee trades. Central America was the Grimaldis' first interest. Their earliest ships were amongst the oldest then afloat, even for these migrant services. First came the 1909-built *Ruahine* of New Zealand Shipping Company which hoisted the Grimaldi flag in 1949. She sailed for eight years as the *Auriga* before being scrapped in 1957. The second ship, even older, was the former Anchor Line *Castalia*, built in 1906. This 6,715-tonner became the

Urania II in 1950. She was broken-up four years later. Their third passenger vessel was the *City of Hong Kong*, a former Ellerman Lines ship dating from 1924. Bought in 1951 and renamed *Centauro*, she made a number of Odessa-South American trips before going to the scrappers in 1955.

The brothers realized, by the early 1950s, however, that the pressing post-War migrant trade with its minimal standards was giving way to more reliable, more comfortable ships. Even the migrants, but especially their government agency sponsors, began to cast a more discerning eye, even to show preferences on the ships they used. And so, when the company bought its fourth passenger ship, the 6,723- ton *Charlton Sovereign* from the Greek-owned Charlton Steam Shipping Company, she was given an extensive and expensive refit.

She had been Canadian National Steamships' *Prince Robert* and then the *Charlton Sovereign*. Recommissioned as the *Lucania*, she carried 170 first class passengers in top-deck comfort and about 800 migrants in much improved third class quarters. She even had two outdoor swimming pools. Highly successful for that time, the 400-foot long, *Lucania* sailed the Italy-Caribbean-Venezuela trade for over ten years until scrapped in 1962. She is shown arriving in this view of Genoa harbor.

Author's collection

The *Ascania* as seen in 1959 before she was modernized and repainted with a black hull. *Maurizio Eliseo collection*

Former Frenchmen

In 1955, the Fratelli Grimaldi paid a little more than $1 million for two French passenger ships that would greatly expand and enhance their passenger ship business, and to take advantage of tax concessions for Sicilian businesses they set up the Palermo-based Sicula Oceanica, the Siosa Lines, as their owners. They even started operating under the name Grimaldi-Siosa Lines, a title that remained until shortened to Siosa Lines in 1962.

The 9,536-ton *Ascania* (there was a 14,400-ton Cunard liner of the same name in service at this time, but she sailed the England-Canada service until late 1956) had been built at St Nazaire in 1926 for Transports Maritimes of Marseilles. As the *Florida,* she sailed between Marseilles and the East Coast of South America. She was, however, very badly damaged in a 1931 collision off Gibraltar with the British aircraft carrier HMS *Glorious.* Later, during the Second World War, she was sunk by the retreating Nazis off Bone, Algeria in November 1944. Salvaged in 1946, she was rebuilt (her original second funnel disappeared in the process) and then returned to the South American run until bought by Grimaldi-Siosa. For her new Italian owners, she was refitted to carry 183 first class and 932 tourist class passengers. She sailed the England-Spain-Portugal-West Indies run. After leaving Southampton, the 14-knot ship called at Vigo, Lisbon and Madeira and then proceeded to the Caribbean: Antigua, St Kitts, Montserrat, Guadeloupe, Martinique, Dominica, St

Lucia, St Vincent, Barbados, Grenada and Trinidad. She then called at La Guaira in Venezuela and sometimes at Curacao. She later returned to Southampton via Kingston and then Maderia, Lisbon and Vigo.

"We carried mostly Spanish and Portuguese and a few Italians on these trips out to the Caribbean," according to Chief Purser Frangini. "The ship was always full and always very crowded. We would have a few first class passengers, maybe a hundred in cabins with private facilities. Tourist class had four-eight berth cabins, none with facilities, and many 60-70 berth dormitories. There wasn't any air-conditioning and many passengers slept out on deck. Some nights, you couldn't walk on the open decks. It was 11-12 days to the West Indies. Of course, ships like the *Ascania* were very old, wearing out. It was a great problem not to have had air-conditioning. A few days each trip were unbearable."

"Venezuela represented great opportunity to many Europeans in those times. In later years, we would actually have family visits back and forth," added Frangini. "We also carried lots of very poor Italians, who were sailing on arranged passages. Some were so poor they could not afford a drink at the bar or even cigarettes. But some passengers actually returned on later voyages because they could not adjust. We also had lots of West Indian children, who were travelling out to visit grandparents in the Caribbean. Many, some two and three year olds, travelled alone with nothing

The *Ascania* again in the early '60s with improvements to her upper decks.   *Roger Sherlock*

more than an identification tag on their arms. They lived in the nursery. Other migrants travelled with enormous baggage, often those big trunks."

"On the return voyages, from the West Indies to the UK, only 50% of the passengers were non-black. We had a few British passengers, but generally the ship was just as full and as crowded in this direction. West Indians were going to the UK for jobs. But the mood could be tense. We needed a master-at-arms, especially for the Jamaicans. We had a few close calls. Once, we even needed to use the hoses." First as assistant purser and then as purser, Ugo Frangini and his staff organized all onboard entertainment on these Grimaldi-Siosa passenger ships. "We had bingo and horse-racing sometimes. The Europeans played lots of cards; the West Indians had lots of domino and scrabble games. The bars onboard were open almost continuously, from seven in the morning until well after midnight. But most passengers could not afford mixed drinks and so we sold mostly soft drinks, coffee and beer. I remember too that the West Indians brought along their own oranges, which I recall were very green. They would suck these constantly."

The *Ascania* also made some North Atlantic crossings, a few between Plymouth, Cherbourg and Quebec City, but she became a budget Mediterranean cruiseship in 1966. She ran seven-day cruises out of Genoa around the western Mediterranean. At forty-two, she was scrapped at La Spezia in 1968.

Although not especially well known to North American travellers, the *Irpinia* was one of the most popular European cruiseships of the 1970s. Her cruises were linked, however, to the European tours of the late Pan American World Airways. The *Irpinia* had a long career, including stints as a trans-Atlantic liner and then, near the end of her days, she even starred in a major motion picture.

The 13,204-ton *Irpinia* was the flagship of Grimaldi-Siosa Lines in the late 1950s. Originally built in 1929, at one of Swan, Hunter's Tyneside yards, she was then owned by the French, by Transports Maritimes (along with the aforementioned *Ascania*). She was named *Campana* and sailed out of Marseilles to the East Coast of South America - to Rio de Janeiro, Santos, Montevideo and Buenos Aires.

After the fall of France in 1940, she was laid-up at Buenos Aires and later seized by the Argentines. For a time, she was called *Rio Jachal* and ran several Buenos Aires-New Orleans sailings for the Argentine State Line. But in 1946, with the War over, she was returned to the French and again sailed to South America as well as on some sailings out to colonial Indochina. She was sold to Grimaldi-Siosa in 1955. She was rebuilt at a Genoa shipyard, being given a raked bow in the process. Her original three-class quarters were rearranged to take 187 in first class and 1,034 in tourist.

She sailed mainly between Europe and the Caribbean, often full to capacity with migrants bound for Venezuela. In 1959-60, however, she spent two summers on a more northern route, sailing between Mediterranean ports, Quebec City and Montreal. She also made periodic trips to New York and once, in 1959,

Above: Perhaps Grimaldi-Siosa's best known early passenger liner, the *Irpinia* originally had two upright funnels and twin masts. *World Ship Society*   *Below:* In 1962, after an extensive refit and re-engining, the *Irpinia* resumed service with a single, tapered funnel and a single mast above the wheelhouse section.   *Alex Duncan*

offered a cruise from New York to La Guaira with return by air. "We carried mostly Hungarian emigrants to Canada," remembered Ugo Frangini. "The *Irpinia* was actually chartered to a relief organization that brought these migrants through Austria to the ports of Genoa and Naples." In 1962, the 537-foot long liner had another facelift. This time, her original twin funnels were replaced by a single tapered stack, new Fiat diesels replaced her original steam turbines and her passenger accommodations were modernized yet again. She returned to the Caribbean route, taking thousands of Spanish and Portuguese migrants and workers westbound, and then West Indian migrants bound for Britain on the return trips. But by 1970, she turned mostly to cruising, usually on week-long runs out of Genoa to Cannes, Barcelona, Palma, Tunis, Palermo and Capri. Then her seven-day voyages were priced from $79; a two-week Christmas-New Year's cruise to the Canary Islands from $134.

In 1976, just as she was to be withdrawn (at the age of forty-seven), she was chartered to a film company for a starring role in "Voyage of the Damned." Two temporary "dummy" stacks were put aboard for her portrayal of the German liner *St. Louis*, which was making its historic 1939 voyage from Germany to Havana with 900 Jewish refugees aboard. "We spent a month at Barcelona - one dock being Germany, another being Havana," recalled Ugo Frangini. "We also went out to sea several times for the sea sequences. All of the actors and the entire film crew lived on the ship. There was James Mason, Faye Dunaway, Lee Grant and Max von Sydow. Miss Dunaway lived in a suite. I especially remember that she never came to the dining room, but ate only caviar and toast washed down with champagne in her rooms. The ship was loaded with all sorts of film equipment, a kind of floating Hollywood studio. They also used Siosa sailors as 'extras'."

After the filming was completed, the *Irpinia*'s owners obviously had some second thoughts about her future. She resumed Mediterranean cruising for several more years, until 1981, by which time she was fifty-two. "She was finally retired because she could no longer get an Italian classification for seaworthiness," added Frangini. Laid-up for two years at La Spezia, she finally met with the wreckers. Her long career was over, but for a few more years some of her furniture and other fittings often appeared in the secondhand shops in and around La Spezia. These were the final links to Italy's *Irpinia*.

Stripped and ready for final scrapping, the *Irpinia* is anchored offshore at La Spezia while awaiting the demolition crews. The year is 1983. *Antonio Scrimali*

Legendary Ladies: the Venezuela and the Caribia

In 1956, in the wake of the *Ascania* and the *Irpinia*, Grimaldi-Siosa purchased its largest liner yet, the 18,769-ton *Venezuela*. She too had an interesting background, having been built in 1924 as the French Line's *De Grasse*, sunk in the War and then salvaged and restored as a modern ship (she now had a single stack instead of the original two). She was sold in 1953, to become Canadian Pacific's *Empress of Australia*, running Liverpool-Montreal sailings. But once in Italian hands, she was sent directly to Genoa and altered for the busy Italy-West Indies-Venezuela migrant and tourist services. Her accommodations were restyled from the 664 total berths onboard the *Empress of Australia* to nearly 1,500 on the *Venezuela*. Berthing was arranged for about 180 in first class, 500 in so-called "tourist cabin"

class and then a further 800 in "tourist minimum". She was also given air-conditioning in all of first class and part of tourist. She entered service in June 1956, on a rather extensive first trip - beginning at Naples, she called at Palermo, Malaga, Vigo, La Guaira, Curacao, Kingston, Vera Cruz, Havana, Port Everglades, Bermuda, Corunna, Santander, Southampton and finally Rotterdam.

The *Venezuela* was a great success, which, in 1960, prompted an extensive overhaul. "She became much more pleasant inside and very modern. There was new furniture, new china, even new blankets," according to Purser Frangini. "A new bow was added (extending her length by 45 feet, to 597 feet overall) both to enhance her looks and increase her service speed (from

Two former North Atlantic liners: The *Venezuela*, shown (*above*) at Lisbon, had been the French Line's *De Grasse* and later Canadian Pacific's *Empress of Australia* (*photo Roger Scozzafava*); the *Caribia* (*below*) had been Italian Line's *Vulcania* in a career that spanned some 45 years.

Steffen Weirauch

The ornate, period stylings of the former *Vulcania* remained when she sailed in cruise service as Siosa's *Caribia*. The first class smoking room and dining room are shown above and below.

Maurizio Eliseo collection

The first class open promenade aboard the *Caribia*.   *Maurizio Eliseo collection*

16 to 18 knots) as well as decrease fuel consumption."

But two years later, the glowing, all-white *Venezuela* was scarred in mud and stained by water damage, a total loss. Ugo Frangini was aboard that fateful voyage out of Genoa bound for the West Indies and Venezuela on March 17, 1962. "We were boarding 200 French West Indians at Cannes when the *Venezuela* stranded. After hitting the rocks, she began to flood. Fortunately, we safely offloaded all the passengers, who then spent a week in Cannes hotels before they could be rebooked on other ships or by air. But the company engineers felt the *Venezuela* was simply too old to repair and so she went prematurely to the scrappers. Just before she was delivered, most of that new furniture, the blankets and even the china were sent over to the *Irpinia*."

She was one of Italy's finest ocean liners - strong and successful, ever popular with passengers as well as crew. Completed in 1928, she sailed as the *Vulcania,* at first for the Cosulich company and then for many years for the Italian Line. Then, for another ten, she was called *Caribia* under the Siosa Lines' houseflag.

The 19-knot *Vulcania* was retired by the Italian Line in the spring of 1965, just as the spectacular pair of *Michelangelo* and *Raffaello* first arrived. But instead of the scrap merchants, she joined Siosa. Renamed *Caribia,* she ran England-Spain-Portugal-West Indies service for a time and later weekly seven-day Mediterranean cruises out of Genoa. Ugo Frangini served aboard her as an assistant purser. "The ship was still very elegant, especially in first class, but she was also very old and very tired. Along with immigrants, we also took many British passengers on month-long,

roundtrip cruises to the Caribbean. But we had lots of problems. The British passengers, for instance, complained about too much soot and smoke from the stack. We gave out lots of refunds in the beginning."

Her subsequent western Mediterranean cruises were very popular and ran Genoa, Cannes, Barcelona, Palma, Bizerta, Palermo and Naples (or sometimes Capri). Minimum fares were $120. But the end for the 44-year-old ship came unexpectedly in September 1972. "At Cannes, during the night and in almost exactly the same spot where the earlier *Venezuela* stranded, the *Caribia*'s old engines failed and a strong northeast wind got hold of her. We lost control," recalled Ugo Frangini. "She drifted onto a reef and had nearly fifty feet of cuts in her hull. And also like the *Venezuela*, she was too old to repair and her marine classification certificate was just about to expire."

The *Caribia* was patched, towed back to Genoa and then sold to scrappers at La Spezia. But her story had not quite ended. A year later, she was resold to Spanish breakers at Barcelona. Then, she was resold again, in 1974, to Taiwanese scrap merchants. She was towed out to the Far East, but that summer, while awaiting a berth at Kaohsiung, she sprang some leaks and flooded. However, she was pumped out and eventually broken up. Ironically, another liner called *Caribia* was also due at Taiwan for scrapping that same summer. The former Cunard cruiseship *Caronia,* she never reached her final destination. While under tow from New York via Panama, she put into Guam and then was thrown onto the rocks by a typhoon and destroyed.

Right: The former Adriatica Line flagship *Ausonia* has been very successfully operated by Siosa Cruises since 1982. A later rebuild gave her this extended after deck. She is due to be retired in 1996.

Antonio Scrimali

Left: The Grimaldis have been long interested in the freighter trades and, in particular, in the auto transport business. The 39,700-ton sisters *Repubblica Di Venezia* and *Repubblica Di Pisa* were built in 1987. But to meet increased trade demands, they were lengthened and given expanded cargo capacities in 1990-1. Their tonnage was increased to 49,000. Quite massive ships, they can carry approximately 55 passengers along with either 1,300 containers or a maximum of 4,480 automobiles. They sail every two weeks between Genoa, Paranagua, Santos and Rio de Janeiro. The *Repubblica Di Venezia* is shown as built in 1987. *A. Molinari*

Right: While similar in purpose, but differing in design (with noticeably separate and higher aft superstructures), two more Grimaldi passenger-cargo liners were added a year or so later, in 1988. The *Repubblica Di Genova* (shown departing from London's Tilbury Docks) was commissioned in July 1988; the *Repubblica Di Amalfi* in the following January. At 35,600 tons, they too had to be 'jumboized' in 1990-91. Their tonnages increased to 42,500. Their current capacities are for 57 passengers and either 1,350 containers or 3,500 cars. These 18-knot ships run a more extensive service, however, one advertised by Grimaldi as the 'Southern Cross Route'. They sail on 6-week round voyages from Northern Europe to West Africa before crossing to Brazil and finally homewards to Europe (either Rotterdam or London is the first port of call). Roundtrip fares were priced from $3,635 in 1993.

Chapter Seven

Flotta Lauro/Starlauro

When Achille Lauro died in November 1982, aged 96, it was the end of an era for post-War Italian passenger shipping. He was the last of the great Italian shipping tycoons who had invested heavily in the old migrant and pre-jet passenger trades. He was also an industrialist and twice mayor of Naples in the 1950s. He was particularly well known for his right wing political views, ones that created many enemies. In fact, his influence was said to be so great and widespread (well beyond his hometown) that he was sometimes called the "King of Naples". As a young man, in 1912, he had inherited a small shipping company from his father. By the mid '50s, he was a multi-millionaire and owner of some ninety ships. But by the 1970s, it was all crumbling. His son Ercole had been placed in charge by then. When the senior Lauro died, there were only seventeen ships left in the fleet and $150 million in debts. The Lauro Line, Flotta Lauro to the Italians, was bankrupt.

"Achille Lauro was said to have had a velvet hand, but a steel arm," according to Captain Antonio Da Rosa, who joined Lauro in 1955 and went on to become master of the company's largest passenger ships. "After the tragic losses of the Second World War, he bought American-built Liberty ships as well as surplus T2 tankers. He built an even bigger shipping empire within ten years. Whenever possible when sailing along the west coast of Italy, we would go close to the seaside near Naples, where Mr Lauro had a residence. We would give three blasts as a salute. But later things went very wrong. It was very sad. Mr Lauro died two years after the collapse of his beloved shipping company."

After the War, and along with reviving his cargo ship fleet, Lauro entered the migrant trades with a converted freighter, the *Ravello* . Within months he needed a second passenger ship and so he added a converted Liberty, the 7,176-ton *Olimpia*. While the *Ravello* had been launched at Genoa in 1941 and then sunk in 1944 before being salvaged and restored, the *Olimpia* had been completed at Jacksonville, Florida in 1943 as the US Government's *James Screven*. The *Ravello* later moved over to the Italy-Venezuela route in 1952 and continued to carry third class passengers until as late as 1960. Then reverting to her original all-cargo status, she was scrapped at La Spezia in 1971. The 11-knot *Olimpia*'s passenger career was comparatively short however. She was converted back to a freighter in 1951 and sailed in Lauro cargo services until broken-up in 1968, also at La Spezia.

Lauro's third early passenger ship was also a converted freighter. The 8,082-ton *Napoli* had been built by Harland & Wolff at Belfast in 1940 as the *Araybank* for Britain's Bank Line. A year later, she was bombed off Crete and abandoned. The Nazis refloated her in 1944 and had her towed to Trieste for restoration. But the project was abandoned once the ship reached Italy and then she was soon in Allied hands. Offered back to the Bank Line in 1945, she was declined. Lauro bought the still badly damaged ship in 1946, had her towed to Muggiano (near La Spezia) and then had her rebuilt with cargo space as well as accommodation for 656 third class passengers (almost 500 of these were housed in large dormitories). She entered service as the *Napoli* in September 1948, but on Lauro's first Australian passenger run - sailing from Genoa and Naples via Suez to Fremantle, Melbourne and Sydney. Actually, she was the first Italian-flag passenger vessel of any kind in the post-War Australian trade. Except for a few homeward evacuation voyages from the troubled East Indies for the Dutch Government, she did not carry passengers on her northbound Lauro sailings.

While these converted cargo ships served an important role in early Lauro passenger history, the company turned to actual passenger ships in May 1949, beginning with the *Surriento*.

In April 1947, the 8,806-ton freighter *Ravello* set off from Naples to Rio de Janeiro, Santos, Montevideo and Buenos Aires. She had been especially refitted to carry third class passengers only. Lauro had secured a contract from the International Refugee Organisation.   *Alex Duncan*

In September 1951, the *Napoli* was rerouted on the South American run. She served there for a little more than a year before being downgraded to all-cargo status for the next twenty or so years. She too was scrapped at La Spezia, in 1971.   *Antonio Scrimali*

Above: Lauro's first full passenger ship was the 10,669-ton *Surriento*, added in May 1949. She had been the Grace Line's *Santa Maria* of 1928, but unusual in American maritime annals for her British construction and Swiss diesels. Lauro bought her at auction after the Second World War and refitted her for the Australian trade (carrying 187 first class, 868 in tourist). She is shown entering Valletta harbor on July 12th 1954. *Michael Cassar*

Below: In 1959, the 498-foot long *Surriento* was given yet another major refit - a new, tapered funnel replaced the original, squat pair (the forward stack had in fact been a 'dummy' and contained the ship's chapel); complete air-conditioning was installed; her public rooms were redone; and all dormitories were removed and replaced by cabins. In 1-6 berth staterooms, her accommodations were rearranged for 1,080 all-tourist class. Now used on the Italy-Caribbean service, she was later briefly chartered to the Zim Lines for Marseilles-Haifa service before going to the breakers in 1966. *Antonio Scrimali*

Having been wartime auxiliary aircraft carriers, the *Sydney* (shown departing from Naples) and her sistership, the *Roma*, were strikingly rebuilt as passenger ships by Lauro in 1949-51. The 14,700-ton pair were routed from Genoa, Naples and Messina to Port Said, Aden, Fremantle, Melbourne and Sydney. Given modern Italian decor, swimming pools and even outdoor cinemas, they carried almost 800 passengers each - just short of 100 in first class and the remainder in tourist. The *Roma* went to the scrappers in 1967 while the *Sydney* was then renamed *Roma* and used for Mediterranean cruising. She was sold to other Italian interests in 1968 and then to the Cypriot-flag Sovereign Cruises in 1970, who renamed her *Galaxy Queen*. She changed hands again in 1972, becoming the *Lady Dina*. She was briefly chartered by Siosa Lines in 1973 as the *Caribia 2* before going to the breakers two years later.

Roger Sherlock

The 23,114-ton *Willem Ruys* was the largest Dutch liner ever to sail in the old colonial East Indies trade.

Roger Sherlock

'The Blue Ship'

Still remembered for her sinister hijacking in October 1985, the *Achille Lauro* was one of the world's most interesting ocean liners. She was a ship of great character, a ship with a colorful background and a ship that almost immediately conveyed a special spirit to those who worked her and sailed her. Her history reached back to that fateful summer of 1939. Then, she was just being built in Holland. She was to be called *Ardjoeno* and was to be the new, luxurious queen on the Rotterdam Lloyd's colonial run out to Batavia (present day Djakarta). But after the Nazis pushed across Dutch soil, her construction was delayed repeatedly. It was not until 1947 that she was finished as the *Willem Ruys*, a name honoring a Rotterdam Lloyd director who had been killed as an enemy hostage.

The *Willem Ruys* remained with the Dutch until 1964 (she was last used in an around-the-world tourist and cruise service), by which time the airlines had cut deeply into her remaining trade. She was sold to Flotta Lauro and thoroughly rebuilt at a Palermo shipyard as the *Achille Lauro*. Her completion was delayed, however, by a fire at the shipyard on August 29, 1965. Just five days before, a fire had swept the *Angelina Lauro* as well, but at a Genoa shipyard. There was extensive damage to both ships and at least six-months delays. It was widely reported that both blazes were acts of sabotage against the politics of their owner, Achille Lauro. But once repaired and then completed in March 1966, the *Achille Lauro* went about her new task: to ferry migrants out from Europe to Australia and New Zealand. "The

Achille Lauro was a very solid ship," according to her long-time master, Captain Antonio Da Rosa. "Her all-riveted hull was very, very strong. She was also a very heavy ship and did well in bad weather."

Her distinctive blue hull coloring gave her several affectionate nicknames such as the "Great Blue Ship." Captain Da Rosa added, "A wealthy Swiss woman wanted to book 'the Blue Ship.' Her agent mistakenly sent her on *The Azur* of Chandris Cruises. She left at the first port and fled to the *Achille Lauro*. She preferred it because of its 'family atmosphere'." The *Achille Lauro* was also one of the few liners with twin smokestacks and these were themselves quite distinctive with a tall, almost tubular effect capped by upwardly slanted, exhaust-deflecting fins. Her lifeboats were also rather unusual, being placed on a far lower deck than on most liners and tucked in an inboard style similar to P&O's big *Canberra*. After rebuilding, her capacity was just about doubled from her earlier Dutch days - to about 1,700 (approximately 270 first class, over 900 in tourist class, nearly 400 interchangeable between first and tourist and a further 150 berths for children under twelve)

"Some passengers waited for as long as ten years before they had an assigned berth on the *Roma* or the *Sydney* and later either the *Achille Lauro* or *Angelina Lauro*," noted Captain Adriano Borreani, who served as a junior officer in these ships. "Some passengers had waited so long and were so old that they actually died. These were migrants, all of them bound for a 'new life'

Above: Vastly changed, the former *Willem Ruys* began sailing as the *Achille Lauro* in 1966.   *Roger Sherlock*

Below: Another Dutch liner, Nederland Line's 20,551-ton *Oranje* , was also rebuilt by Lauro in 1964-65. Built at Amsterdam in 1939, she had been the fastest passenger ship ever to ply the Amsterdam-Djakarta run. Lauro renamed her *Angelina Lauro*.   *Eric Johnson*

in far-off Australia. There were Yugoslavians, Austrians, Poles, Hungarians and lots and lots of Italians. But this was not the sea travel of a century ago, but of the 1960s and early 1970s. Historically, these were some of the last migrants to go by sea."

"We had 70-day roundtrips," added Captain Borreani, "that sailed from Bremerhaven, Rotterdam, Southampton, Genoa, Naples, Messina, Malta and sometimes Beirut through the Suez Canal to Fremantle, Melbourne and Sydney. After, we usually did a small cruise over to New Zealand with mostly young Australians. These were very cheap voyages and mostly full-up."

"On the outbound Australian trips, we were always packed - sometimes as many as 1,735 in all. There were British mostly in first class and then all the mixed nationalities in tourist class. Many of these migrants had their fares paid for them, usually by the Australian Government under the resettlement plan. Many of them had no luggage. Some were pregnant, even past three months. Once, a Lebanese couple had their baby onboard. She was named Laura for Lauro."

The summer trips in June, July and August, were the most trying according to Captain Borreani. "The Indian Ocean monsoons caused a great deal of sea-sickness. Many passengers were petrified and it was impossible to persuade them to leave their cabins, and we had so many languages, it was impossible to communicate. With the Yugoslavians in particular, we had to use hand language. But when these passengers were well, they ate anything and everything. If one of them died onboard, we usually buried them at sea, especially if the family had no money. We always did this at two in the morning, without other passengers seeing it."

Like the *Achille Lauro*, the *Angelina Lauro* was delayed by a shipyard fire in August 1965 while being rebuilt for the Australian trade. But once in service, she was a greatly changed ship with her raked bow, single mast atop the wheel-house and a winged funnel. After 1973, she turned to cruising fulltime and was operated in her final years by the Costa Line.   *Roger Sherlock*

"There was always a representative of the Australian Government onboard looking after the needs of these migrants. They gave talks on Australian life and held classes on important English words. The various groups usually had one English-speaking person as a relay. Landing in Australia was highly organised. Migrants who did not have homes to go to were sent to relocation centres and were given jobs, usually manual. However, by the 1970s general migration virtually ceased. All the big Mediterranean passenger firms - Lauro, Lloyd Triestino, Sitmar and Chandris - lost the main part of their business."

A galley fire finished off the *Angelina Lauro* during a Caribbean cruise on March 30th 1979. The ship was ruined. Scorched and then flooded with fire-fighters' water, she was declared a total loss. With a 25-degree list, she was not salvaged until that July and then sold to Taiwanese scrap merchants.

Author's collection

Both the *Achille Lauro* and her fleetmate, the *Angelina Lauro*, were restyled as cruiseships by 1973. By then, the era of Australian migrant trips was just about over. With her capacity reduced to about 900 all one-class, the *Achille Lauro* spent most of her year in the Mediterranean and then, in winter, made one, long, luxury cruise (around-the-world, around South America, the Far East). But Lauro eventually fell on hard financial times. Returning from South Africa in January 1982, the *Achille Lauro* was arrested for debt when she reached Tenerife. Her passengers were stranded and the ship was left with only a maintenance staff for a year. The Italian Government brought the ship to Genoa in January 1983, where she continued in lay-up until revived, in July 1984, in a joint charter agreement between a greatly diminished Lauro and Chandris Cruises. She ran two-week cruises from Genoa mostly. After the hijacking in October 1985, Chandris withdrew as the ship's popularity slumped. Despite rumors that she would be sold or at least renamed, Lauro ran her until 1987. But with Mediterranean cruising in an enormous slump, primarily due to her hijacking and other terrorist events in the area, she carried fewer and fewer passengers. She was also in need of remodelling as well as repairs. Her owners were just about bankrupt once again when, in 1987, the Swiss-based Mediterranean Shipping Company bought the ship and reorganized her operations as Starlauro Cruises. Upgraded and improved, she continued to cruise mostly in the Mediterranean.

Very sadly, on November 30, 1994, while on a cruise from Genoa to South Africa via Suez, the *Achille Lauro* caught fire while at sea off Somalia. Abandoned, she sank two days later.

The *Angelina Lauro* left St Thomas under tow for Kaohsiung on July 30th 1979. But her troubles continued as the empty ship began to take on water in mid-Pacific two months later, on September 21st. On the 25th, the 40-year-old liner rolled over and sank.   *Andy Hernandez collection*

Above: For summer cruising in the Mediterranean, Lauro chartered several passenger ships in the late 1970s and early '80s. Among these were the *Cunard Princess*, the *Daphne* and the *Oceanos* of Epirotiki Lines (seen above temporarily wearing the Lauro star on her funnel). *Alex Duncan*

Below: In 1989, the former American cruiseship *Monterey* joined Lauro, which was then under new ownership and renamed Starlauro Cruises. A former freighter built in 1952 and then rebuilt for the Matson Line's California-South Pacific service in 1956, she has since cruised the Mediterranean and the Caribbean for her Italian operators. She is owned by the Mediterranean Shipping Company, the parent of Starlauro, and flies the Panamanian flag. She has a maximum capacity of 661 passengers. In September 1994 a further ship was added to the Starlauro fleet - the Costa Line's *Enrico Costa*. She was to have been refitted before entering service but, in the aftermath of the *Achille Lauro* tragedy, she was hurriedly sent to South Africa to take up that ship's intended schedule. Now with the famous Lauro star on her funnel, she is called the *Symphony*. At the same time Starlauro Cruises changed their name to Star Cruises. Then, within weeks, another ship was bought. She is the former *Cunard Princess* which is now called *Rhapsody*. *Alex Duncan*

Chapter Eight

Home Lines

Early History & Early Ships

"Home Lines was born soon after the War, in early 1946, and was a combination of the Swedish American Line, the Cosulich Company (the same Italian family who owned such pre-War liners as the *Saturnia* and the *Vulcania*) and a Greek shipowner, Mr Eugen Eugenides." So recalled Captain Mario Vespa, who worked for the old Cosulich Line in the 1920s and '30s, and then served the Home Lines for nearly forty years, beginning in 1946. The Home Lines was, in fact, an early combination of two now largely forgotten passenger firms - the Panamanian Lines, which was managed by the Cosulich interests out of Trieste, and the South Atlantic Lines, owned partly by Swedish American. Officially, these two companies were merged in 1952 to become the Mediterranean Lines and then, soon afterwards, the Home Lines. The original connection to the Swedish

our *Italia,* and the *Drottningholm,* which we renamed *Brasil.*"

Today, involved in the ship brokerage, chartering and bunkering businesses, the 88-year-old Captain Vespa works full weeks at his New York City offices. Located on the upper floors of a midtown Art Deco tower, the quarters are expectedly old style: cramped, cluttered, a miniature museum. Bookcases, overloaded desks and well-stocked tables fill out much of the floor space. The walls are lined with reminders of the Captain's long career: paintings of ships such as the *Saturnia* and the *Hanseatic,* harbor photos, groups of those maiden voyage publicity scenes and signed photos of various Cosulich family members. A huge service award given to Captain Vespa in the late 1970s is signed by the chief officer of every passenger ship company then operating in the United States. Scale models abound as well - larger ones of ships such as the old *Homeland* and the *Italia,* and then other, smaller

Home Lines' first passenger ship was the *Argentina,* the former *Bergensfjord,* built in 1913 for the Norwegian America Line.

Alex Duncan

American Line was always best seen in the very similar funnel markings - while the SAL liners bore three golden crowns on each funnel, Home Lines' ships had only one, but large crown. "Our first ship," Captain Vespa added, "was the old *Bergensfjord,* which had been owned by the Norwegians, but used by the British in the War. She was renamed *Argentina.* Then, from our Swedish American partner, we took over two of their ships - the former *Kungsholm* (used by the Americans in War service as the USS *John Ericsson*), which became

replicas of the *Oceanic,* the *Homeric* and the *Doric.* The phones rang often and one call actually interrupted our interview. A journalist wanted to interview Captain Vespa because of his "slight involvement" in the SS *United States* revival project. While usually optimistic on that subject, he declined on that afternoon in November 1993. "We called our company the Home Lines, a formation of the word 'holm' from the Swedish, meaning 'home'," the Captain added. "We were named on January 9, 1946. Our primary trade was migrants -

Italians and Central Europeans (Poles, Czechs, Austrians and Germans) - going to South America. Immigration laws were much easier then. In return, we carried a few visitors, tourists if you will, going to Europe. They were usually in first and second class."

The 11,000-ton *Argentina*, built back in 1913 by Cammell Laird's at Birkenhead, had been part of the first pair of passenger ships for the then new Norwegian America Line fleet. Called *Bergensfjord*, she had sailed the North Atlantic - trading between Oslo, Copenhagen, Bergen, Kristiansand, Halifax and New York.

The *Bergensfjord* was called to War duties in 1940, but under British control (Furness Withy handled her management). She survived unscathed. She was, however, too old for Norwegian restoration by 1946 and so was sold to the Home Lines. She was refitted at Genoa with a restyled berthing pattern for a mere 32 in first class and 969 in tourist. She sailed as the *Argentina*, flying the Panamanian flag, between Naples, Genoa, Rio, Santos, Montevideo and Buenos Aires. So successful, she was soon joined by the *Brasil* and then the *Italia*. Panamanian Lines also ran some South American and other migrant sailings using the 7,700-ton *Protea*. But this ship was never considered to be a part of the Home Lines' fleet. A converted former American freighter, she later went on the Australian trade and then was sold to become the Arosa Line's *Arosa Kulm*. She was scrapped in 1959.

"But we had huge problems in 1949," added Captain Vespa. "In particular, the devaluation of the Argentine peso ended it all. Migrant service dwindled. Our passenger service to South America was no longer possible and so the Cosulichs diverted the *Argentina* to Caribbean service and the others to New York, in a service that was like the 1920s and '30s with the old *Saturnia* and the *Vulcania*."

While briefly later used on the New York run, the aged *Argentina* was sold in 1953 to the then infant Zim Israel Navigation Company, the Zim Lines. She was renamed *Jerusalem* and, that April, opened the Company's Haifa-New York trans-Atlantic service. Two years later, being replaced by the brand new combination passenger-cargo liners *Israel* and *Zion*, the 530-foot long *Jerusalem* was kept in Mediterranean waters, sailing between Marseilles, Genoa, Naples and Haifa. Renamed *Aliya* in 1957, her days were numbered when it was rumored that she was to become a hotel ship in Belgium for the 1958 World's Fair at Brussels. That never materialized and, she was finally laid-up in May 1958, after 45 busy years of service. A year later, she went to the breakers at La Spezia.

Italia (1928)

The Swedish American Line sold its famed pre-War trans-Atlantic and cruising liner *Kungsholm*, built by Blohm & Voss at Hamburg in 1928, to the US Government just after the attack on Pearl Harbor, in January 1942. She became the troopship USS *John*

Being a major partner in Home Lines, the Swedish American Line provided two of that company's early passenger ships. The *Italia*, the former *Kungsholm* of 1928, is shown leaving Malta in 1949.   *Roger Sherlock*

In 1948, Captain Vespa travelled from Italy to San Francisco, a considerable journey in those post-war years, to meet with the Matson Line in their downtown offices. "Their *Matsonia* was for sale", acording to Captain Vespa. "The ship was in good condition and, of course, was of the most impeccable standard of construction. American liners have always been very sound investments. They are easy to convert, they are safe and they go on forever! But we had one big stipulation from the US Government: Such ships could not compete with American-flag liners. We could only spend a few months each year out of US ports. But we bought this Matson ship for our then booming Italy-South America service. We brought the *Matsonia* through the Panama Canal and then over to Genoa (to the Ansaldo shipyard). She came back as the *Atlantic*". Built in 1927 at Philadelphia as the *Malolo* and then renamed *Matsonia* in 1937, she actually went directly into Italy-New York service for the Home Lines in the Spring of 1949 and later in North Europe-Eastern Canada service. She joined a Home Lines' subsidiary, the National Hellenic American Line, in 1954 and became the *Queen Frederica*. A decade later, she joined Chandris and sailed for them until laid-up in 1973. She was scrapped in 1977-78 after a career of 50 years.

Everett Viez collection

Ericsson, managed by the United States Lines for the old War Shipping Administration. After the hostilities, in March 1947, she was badly damaged by fire while berthed at Cunard's Pier 90 (just across from the mighty *Queen Elizabeth*) at New York. Having no further use for her now, the Americans sold her back to her original Swedish owners, who then promptly resold her to the Home Lines (the South Atlantic Lines). She went to Ansaldo's Genoa yard and was refitted as the *Italia*. The 21,554-ton ship became one of Home Lines' most successful and most popular liners.

The 609-foot long *Italia* started Italy-South America sailings in July 1948. She joined the *Argentina* and the *Brasil*. But such a trio was rather shortlived. In June 1949, prompted by those severe currency problems in Latin America and the consequent drop in westbound migrant traffic, the Home Lines turned its attention to the North Atlantic and, in particular, to the New York trades. The *Italia* made her first sailings between Genoa, Naples, Barcelona, Lisbon and New York. Her accommodations were arranged in three classes - 226 in first class, 296 in cabin class and 800 in tourist. However, this was altered to 120 first and 1,320 tourist by 1952.

"Coming to New York was a bit of a gamble," remembered Captain Vespa. "We were unknown and there was considerable competition back then." Competition came from the likes of the brand new American sisterships *Independence* and *Constitution,* and later from an equally splendid pair from Italy, the *Andrea Doria* and the *Cristoforo Colombo*. Home Lines finally had to reconsider its place in the Mediterranean-New York trade. They saw greater potential and a greater opening in North European service, in particular filling the void left by the still passenger ship - inactive Hamburg America Line (and even the slowly reawakening North German Lloyd). So, starting in March 1952, the *Italia* began regular sailings between Hamburg, Southampton, Halifax and New York. "The Home Lines had been approached by Hamburg America to re-establish German trans-Atlantic service," noted Captain Vespa. "The idea seemed practical and was accepted immediately. Eventually, this led to a joint formation, in 1957, of the Hamburg-Atlantic Line for Hamburg-New York service under the West German flag. We bought the *Empress of Scotland* and rebuilt her as the *Hanseatic*. It was all very successful - to an extent."

By 1959, the *Italia* was replaced by the *Hanseatic* in American service and so was reassigned to the Canadian trade. Cuxhaven replaced Hamburg, and Quebec City and Montreal replaced Halifax and New York. But still more changes were ahead. In less than two years, beginning in December 1960, the *Italia* was selected to become Home Lines' experimental ship: a year-round cruiseship running continuous cruises between New York and Nassau. She sailed every Saturday afternoon at four o'clock and then returned the following Saturday morning at eight. Minimum fare was $170. She was a gamble that turned into a huge success and, in fact, was a forerunner of the huge American cruise industry of today.

"Home Lines was fascinated by the old *Nassau*, which ran seven-day New York-Nassau cruises for another Italian-style company, the Incres Line," remembered Captain Vespa. "The *Nassau*'s success prompted our decision to use the superior *Italia* in the same service. We took a chance. A shipping magazine called the decision 'madness,' but then apologized a year later. It was a step in the dark. After all, we were not a selective ship like, say, the *Caronia*."

In addition to her seven-day voyages to Nassau and back, the *Italia* would make an annual autumn cruise to the Mediterranean (coordinated with her yearly overhaul). She also ran occasional ten-day cruises from New York, calling at Nassau and perhaps Port-au-Prince, and later winter cruises from Port Everglades. She was withdrawn in April 1964, just as the brand new *Oceanic* was coming into service. While the veteran ship was rumored to become a Home Lines' Mediterranean cruiseship or an Australian migrant ship, she was sold to an investment group, Freeport Bahama Enterprises. Renamed *Imperial Bahama Hotel*, she was sent to Freeport, then a fledgling resort on Grand Bahama Island. Her future seemed assured, but instead she was snared in financial problems, corruption and then bankruptcy. Seized by local authorities, she was auctioned-off to Spanish shipbreakers and, in late summer 1965, was towed across to Bilbao and scrapped.

Brasil/Homeland

The 11,182-ton *Brasil* made her first Home Lines' sailing in July 1948, casting off from Genoa for ports along the East Coast of South America. But she too had to find alternative work - first in Mediterranean-New York service and then, starting in June 1951, in Home Lines' new North Atlantic service. Renamed *Homeland* just before her inaugural crossing from Hamburg to New York, she was reconditioned as well, now carrying 96 in upper-deck first class quarters and 846 in tourist. "The *Homeland* was actually bareboat chartered to the Hamburg America Line," according to German maritime historian Arnold Kludas. "Homes Lines even offered to sell the ship to Hapag (as Hamburg America was called). While actually registered in Panama, she flew both the Home Lines and Hamburg America house flags. She had a Hapag captain and Hapag hired most of the crew. She carried migrants to Canada (Halifax) and New York. They were mostly Germans. In return, she carried Germans on returning visits, most of whom had not been in the country since before the War."

Built in Scotland back in 1905, the old *Homeland* had started her career as the *Virginian* for the Glasgow-based Allan Line. She and her sistership, the *Victorian*, are noteworthy in ocean liner history. They were the first steam turbine liners on the Atlantic. The *Virginian* went on to join the Canadian Pacific during the First World War and then hoisted the Swedish American Line colors in 1920, becoming their *Drottningholm*. She sailed in Atlantic service between Gothenburg, Copenhagen and New York. During the Second World War, she served as an exchange ship for the

One of the most enduring of trans-Atlantic passenger ships, the *Homeland* - the former Swedish American *Drottningholm* - had a career that spanned 50 years.

Home Lines

International Red Cross. Restored, she resumed her Swedish American service in 1946 before joining the Home Lines two years later.

After exactly fifty years of sailing, the *Homeland* was sold to Italian scrappers at Trieste in March 1955.

"Axel Bitsch-Christensen worked for the Home Lines at that time," Arnold Kludas recalls. "But he later formed his own company (in 1957), called the Hamburg Atlantic Line. Mr Eugenides had given him six million DM. Hapag were involved as the managers of their first ship, the converted *Hanseatic*. However, the collaboration between the Home Lines and Hamburg Atlantic ended in September 1966, when the *Hanseatic* burned at New York. Afterwards, a new company was formed, the German Atlantic Line, with a 'new' *Hanseatic* and the brand new *Hamburg*."

Captain Vespa returned to San Francisco in 1953 to buy a second Matson liner. "I met with the husband of Lurline Matson", he recalled, "and bought the liner *Mariposa*, which had been laid-up since the end of the Second World War. The entire sale was arranged in a San Francisco restaurant. The actual details were written on the back of a menu!" Renamed *Homeric* and rebuilt to carry 147 first class and 1,096 tourist class passengers, she was delivered in January 1955 (shown departing from Trieste on her maiden crossing to New York). Used in North Europe-Canada service, mainly from Southampton, she went into fulltime cruising in late 1963. She was very popular.

Everett Viez collection

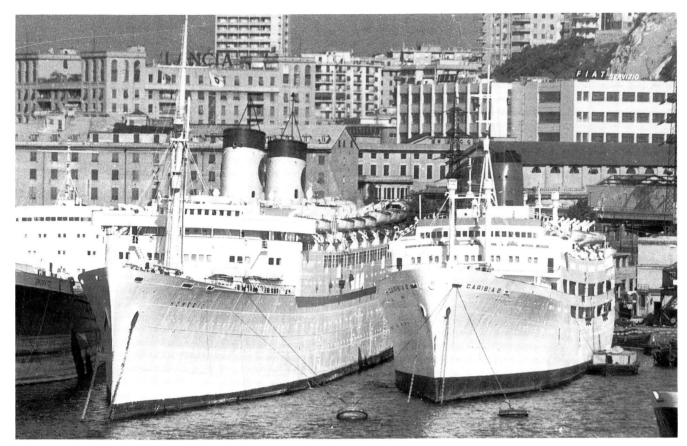

Damaged by fire off the New Jersey coast in July 1973, the *Homeric* (left) was laid-up at Genoa a month later and is shown moored alongside the *Caribia 2*. Both were destined for the breakers - the *Homeric* in Taiwan, the *Caribia 2* at nearby La Spezia.

Antonio Scrimali

The Fabulous Oceanic

"Whenever I saw her, in the 1970s and '80s, I thought she was the most fantastic ship. She was beautiful to look at - a real ship, by today's standards. She was also very well known, gave superb performance, had high speed and behaved beautifully in bad weather." So recalled Captain Dimitrios Chilas, who later became her first master when she joined

Florida's Premier Cruise Lines in October 1985. Unquestionably, the 39,200-ton *Oceanic* was one of the very finest passenger ships of her time, built in that grand heyday of Italian shipbuilding of the 1960s. She was also the Home Lines' largest, fastest and most luxurious ship to date as well as their very first newbuilding. "She was a most important ship, one of the very finest ever," added Captain Vespa. "We designed her to do as much as 27 knots on the North

Right: With her engines-aft design, retractable glass covering over her swimming pools and her splendid contemporary decor, the *Oceanic* was one of the most outstanding ocean liners of the 1960s.

Everett Viez collection

Atlantic, to do Southampton to Quebec in five days flat. But then, of course, she became the greatest cruiseship of her time." She was built by Cantieri Riuniti dell'Adriatico at Monfalcone, practically alongside the even larger *Raffaello* and then the later *Eugenio C.* Home Lines had ordered the 1,600-passenger ship in 1960 for the final era of their North Atlantic service. It was planned that she would be the finest liner on the Canadian run, sailing from Cuxhaven (for Hamburg), Le Havre and Southampton over to Quebec and Montreal for about eight months of the year. In deep winter, she would cruise from New York to the Caribbean. But by the fall of 1963, and with the intended two-class liner well under construction, Home Lines decided to drop all Atlantic crossings in favour of year-round cruising. Both the veteran *Italia* and *Homeric* had been immensely successful in the seven-day New York-Nassau cruise trade as well as in longer West Indian voyages, but there had never been a ship as large as the 774-foot long *Oceanic* in weekly cruising out of New York. Then amongst the finest, best operated cruise companies in the world, Home

Caribbean cruises were far more formal," according to Len Chapman, who joined Home Lines as a junior purser in 1974. "Everything revolved around the passengers on these cruises. It was all top-shelf. We provided the best service. For example, we had 'night stewards', elderly gentlemen who had been with Home Lines for over twenty years. The Italian cuisine and service was legendary. Great quality was given and expected. Great attention was paid to every last detail and the passengers were more experienced, more demanding. Even the sailing days were great occasions. There would be gala bon voyage parties in the suites and cabins that included champagne and those great trays of canapes. Friends brought flowers and baskets of fruit and cookies. Then there was a high spirited departure with paper streamers draped between the ship and the pier. Of the 800 or so passengers, 600 were repeaters. Everyone practically knew everyone else. We even carried a social columnist on these winter cruises."

Years later, when she was being replaced by the new *Homeric*, there were rumors that she might be bought

In the colors of Premier Cruise Lines, the *Starship Oceanic* is seen at Nassau in February 1994. The following winter she had a major refit in Italy.   *Author's collection*

Lines decided to gamble. The *Oceanic*'s success was beyond even their wildest expectations. In her first season on the weekly Nassau run (minimum fares started at $175), she was booked continuously to 98% of capacity. She had arrived in New York for the first time in April 1965, to fireboat and tugboat escorts, overhead helicopters and then a round of celebratory luncheons, dinners and other receptions. There was even a novelty to the occasion: as the gleaming *Oceanic* sailed along the Hudson for the first time, she was followed by a second cruiseship, Norway's *Viking Princess* (the former Italian *Riviera Prima*), which was also on her maiden call at New York. (Interestingly, there were persistent rumours just two years later that *Oceanic* would be sold to the Holland America Line to replace their mechanically troubled *Nieuw Amsterdam*. But while such a sale seems unlikely, the *Oceanic* could have been refitted to her original two-class configuration in place of the then 29-year old Dutch liner.) While she ran her weekly Nassau cruises 'from April thru December', she went deeper into the Caribbean in winter, on 12-19 day cruises. Then her capacity was reduced to about 800 (from the 1,200 maximum on the seven-day sailings). "These

by Chandris Fantasy Cruises. However, she was finally sold to Premier. She would go into the overnight Florida-Bahamas trade, sailing alongside Premier's first ship, the *Royale*, Costa's former *Federico C.* "The *Oceanic* was delivered to us at Norfolk and then had a long refit before she started cruising for Premier in April 1986," noted Captain Chilas. "Repainted with a bright red hull, Premier's affiliation with Disney World at Orlando (the ship sailed from nearby Port Canaveral) led to her new identity as the 'Mickey Mouse ship'. I took her to Boston in September 1987 for a two-week charter to the Digital Computer Company. She served as an exposition ship together with the *QE2*. While going north, we hit rough seas off Cape Hatteras. But she performed so well. We were even two hours early into Boston. I was so proud of this great ship. Later, in December 1987, we ran a long Christmas Caribbean cruise. We steamed direct from Port Canaveral to San Juan at 24.5 knots, using one ton of fuel for every mile steamed! She still has some of the largest cabins afloat and some of the original Italian artwork. But she is all new in other ways, a completely different ship. I used to think what it would be like to be captain of the *Oceanic*. It was as exciting as I expected."

Above: Home Lines added the *Doric* in early 1974 (shown arriving at New York that March with the *Michelangelo* in the foreground). Built in 1964, she had been Zim Line's *Shalom* and then German Atlantic Line's *Hanseatic*. She was later sold to Royal Cruise Lines in 1981 and was rebuilt with a single funnel as their *Royal Odyssey*. In 1988, she became Regency Cruises' *Regent Sun*.

   Moran Towing & Transportation Company

Right: To replace the *Doric* Home Lines turned to the French, the CNIM shipyards at La Seyne, the builders of such ships as the exquisite *Sagafjord*. Launched in January 1981, the 672-foot long liner was commissioned in April 1982 (shown here arriving in New York for the first time) as the *Atlantic*. But when Holland America Line bought out Home Lines in April 1988, the *Atlantic* was soon sold to Premier Cruise Lines and became their *Starship Atlantic*.

   Flying Camera Inc.

The 42,092-ton *Homeric*, completed in May 1986 and shown departing from New York on October 17th 1987, proved to be Home Lines' final passenger ship. Built to replace the earlier *Oceanic*, she joined Holland America in the fall of 1988 and became their *Westerdam*. Lengthened a year later, she currently measures 53,872 tons.

Neil McGuinness

Chapter Nine
Cogedar Line

Cogedar was an acronym for one of those long, very official Italian corporate names: Compagnia Genovese d'Armamento. Genoa-based, they had already carried passengers to South America in temporarily converted freighters when, in 1948, they introduced the 7,964-ton *Genova*. Built in 1922 as an American freighter, the *Missourian*, she had served the British and then the Belgians during the Second World War. The Italians rebuilt her in 1948 as a passenger ship with a capacity for 860 all-third class. She plied the Italy-South America run. "She was an uncomfortable ship," recalled Captain Elvio Arimondo, then a young cadet onboard. "She was not the best 'sea boat' and so quite fortunately we never hit any really bad weather on these South Atlantic crossings. After landing passengers at Rio, Santos, Montevideo and Buenos Aires, we dismantled their bunks in the holds and used the space to carry meats, cheeses and beans back to Italy."

Rebuilt and re-engined in 1955 as the *Flaminia*, the 14-knot ex-*Genova* was then placed on the Australian run. Her voyages were later extended to Northern Europe, to include Bremerhaven, Rotterdam and Southampton. The aged ship was chartered to the Zim Lines in 1962, running sailings between Marseilles and Haifa. Soon thereafter, she was sold to Arab buyers, the Saudi Lines, and became the Moslem pilgrim ship *King Abdelaziz*. She was scrapped in Taiwan in 1970. In this view, she is shown berthed at Genoa in 1961.

Antonio Scrimali

Cogedar's second passenger ship was the 10,480-ton *Aurelia*, which was added in 1954 for the Australian and later around-the-world tourist trades. She had been the *Huascaran*, built in 1939 for the Hamburg America Line's West Coast of South America run and then, after the War, she became Canadian Pacific's *Beaverbrae*, ferrying migrants on westward passages to Canada and then returning as a freighter. The 1,124-passenger ship sailed in Cogedar's Australian service until 1968, when they tried her in British cruise service. Unsuccessful, she went to Chandris in 1970 and became their *Romanza*. They sold her in 1991 to Cypriot buyers, Ambassador Leisure Cruises, who sail her as the *Romantica* on 3-and 4-day cruises between Cyprus, Israel and Egypt. *Victor Scrivens collection*

When Cunard decided to retire their 250-passenger combination liner *Media* in 1961, she found a buyer almost immediately. Cogedar brought her to a Genoa shipyard and had her rebuilt as the 1,220-passenger *Flavia*. Competing with a new generation of migrant ships on the Australian run, she was especially fitted with all modern amenities; complete air-conditioning, swimming pools, modern public rooms and special children's facilities. Most of her cabins had private shower and toilet. She entered service in December 1962. But as Cogedar's trade was winding down, she was transferred to the Costa Line in 1968 and placed in Florida-Bahamas cruise service. She remained there until 1982 when she went to Hong Kong owners, becoming *Flavian*, the *Lavia* and finally the *Lavian*. Laid-up mostly, she was undergoing repairs for a return to cruise service when, on January 7th 1989, she caught fire and later capsized in Hong Kong harbor. She was soon scrapped on nearby Taiwan. She was Cogedar's largest liner and their last.

Roger Sherlock

Chapter Ten
Other Italians & Near-Italians

A number of other, lesser known Italian-controlled companies, often using foreign flags, tried to cash in on the huge post-War migrant business. All sorts of ships, some quite ancient, were despatched on a variety of runs: to South America, the West Indies, Australia, Africa and the North Atlantic. Genoese shipowner Ignazio Messina ran the 6,900-ton *Lugano,* a former British freighter dating from 1898, and the *Pace,* the former American cruiseship *Cuba.* Societa Anonima Cooperativa di Navigazione Garibaldi ran several converted passenger ships or former freighters including the *Marengo* and the *Luciano Manara.* Sidarma (for Societa Italiana d'Armamento) ran two converted freighters, the *Andrea Gritti* and the *Francesco Morosini* while another Italian cargo company, Italnavi, ran their *Sestriere* and *Sises.*

While Italians manned and staffed them, three other early migrant ships flew the Panamanian as a "flag of convenience." The 5,426-ton *Roma* was listed to Compania Naviera San Miguel (and later became Costa's *Franca C.*). The slightly larger 7,474-ton *Liguria* was listed to Compania Naviera Baru and the third, the 7,821-ton *Florentia,* belonged to Compania de Navegacion Florencia. The *Florentia* had been the *Burma,* built in 1914 for the Glasgow-based Henderson Line. Between 1949 and 1953, she ran Italy-Australia sailings before becoming the Moslem pilgrim ship *Safina-E-Nusrat* for Pakistan's Pan-Islamic Steamship Company. She went to Karachi breakers in September 1957.

The *Roma* and the *Liguria* sailed to Australia and also on trans-Atlantic charters for the Roman Catholic Holy Year of 1950. Joan Duffy was a passenger aboard both ships that year. "The National Council of Catholic College Students chartered the *Roma* and the *Liguria* to take hundreds of us to Rome. When we boarded the *Liguria* in Hoboken, we were shocked to discover that the entire hold of the ship had been cleared to make way for a huge dormitory of double-decker bunk beds. There were very few actual staterooms onboard either ship. The six-week trip using the ships cost each of us $549. The Atlantic crossing took ten days each way. Our group returned late because the *Liguria* broke down. The dining rooms were pleasant, but the food was awful."

Laid down in 1914 as the *Hilda Woermann* for the German-flag Woermann Line, the *Liguria* spent the 1920s and '30s as the Australian-owned *Marella.* In 1948, she went to the Italians, the Lloyd Genovese, and sailed for a short time as the *Captain Marcos.* She became the *Liguria* in 1950, certified to carry 929 all-third class passengers. A later, Australian sailing was marred by both mechanical and financial problems and the ship was arrested for debt at Fremantle. She later became the *Corsica.* Laid-up by 1952, she was sold to Belgian shipbreakers two years later.

The trouble-plagued *Liguria.*   *Author's collection*

Above: It should be mentioned that the Ansaldo shipyard at Genoa built three fine combination liners - the *Rio de la Plata*, the *Rio Jachal* (shown at New York on her maiden arrival in September 1950) and the *Rio Tunuyan* - for the New York-East Coast of South America service of the Argentine State Line. Along with cargo capacity, they had all-first class quarters for 116 passengers. Their round voyages were offered as 43-day cruises. While the earlier two were damaged in separate fires and later scrapped during the 1960s, the *Rio Tunuyan* spent several years in North European service before being broken-up herself in 1972.

Argentine State Line

Below: Formed in 1950, the Incres Line was Italian owned, but used New York as its headquarters. The line was the creation of the Genoese shipowner Paolo Scerni. Incres was his family anagram! Incres was amongst the very first New York passenger lines to use a 'flag of convenience' to avoid both costly taxes and strict regulations. They used the Panama flag and later, after 1954,

the Liberian colors. Their first ship was an ex-P&O liner, a 15,000-tonner that they had used briefly in North Atlantic service as the *Europa*. But within less than a year, by 1951, she was refitted as the cruiseship *Nassau*. She had been P&O's *Mongolia* and later New Zealand Shipping Company's *Rimutaka*. She spent most of her Incres days in New York-Nassau service, but made occasional extended trips (including one to London for the Coronation in June 1953 where she is shown at Tilbury). She was sold to the Mexicans, to their Natumex Line, in 1961 and further refitted as the *Acapulco*. But unsuccessful, she was sold to Japanese scrappers in late 1964. *Roger Sherlock*

Above: Incres expanded to a second cruiseship in 1959 when they added the former Union-Castle *Dunnottar Castle*, originally built in 1936 and now extensively rebuilt as the 600-passenger *Victoria*. Popular in mostly New York-Caribbean service, she and her owners were sold to Sweden's Clipper Line in 1964. A decade or so later, in 1975, Incres fell into bankruptcy and the ship itself was later auctioned off to Chandris Cruises. She ran as *The Victoria* for them until 1992, when she joined the Cypriot-flag Louis Cruise Lines, who sail her as the *Princesa Victoria* on 3- and 4-day cruises between Cyprus, Israel and Egypt.   *Incres Line*

Below: The 12,000-ton combination liner *Lavoisier* was built at St Nazaire in 1948 for France's Chargeurs Reunis. She was used on their North Europe-East Coast of South America run, carrying considerable freight as well as 94 first class and 230 tourist class passengers. She was sold to the Italians in 1961, to Commerciale Marittima Petroli, based at Palermo, and rebuilt at Genoa as the

600-passenger cruiseship *Riviera Prima.* Her maiden voyage was a Mediterranean cruise in July 1962. But thereafter, she did considerable charter cruising for an American firm called Caribbean Cruise Lines. But when they suddenly went bankrupt in the summer of 1964, the ship quickly disembarked her final passengers and 'fled' from New York for Italy and the safety of her owners. Unable to secure any further charters, she was sold to the Norwegians, to Berge Sigval Bergesen & Company, in October 1964 and became their *Viking Princess* for US-Caribbean service. But this new career was quite brief. In April 1966, she caught fire off Cuba and had to be abandoned. Her blistered hull was later placed under tow and delivered to Spanish breakers.

Vincent Messina collection

As Miami-Caribbean cruising blossomed in the early 1970s, the Norwegian Caribbean Lines ordered a pair of 17,000-ton sisterships, the *Southward* and the *Seaward*, from the Cantieri Navali del Tirreno shipyards at La Spezia. The 770-passenger *Southward* was delivered in December 1971. However, the *Seaward* project was abandoned just after Italian shipyards were nationalized and her construction costs suddenly jumped by 50 per cent. Nevertheless the ship was completed, but with modifications, as the *Spirit of London* for the P&O Lines. Soon renamed *Sun Princess* (shown), she was assigned to P&O's Princess Cruises division, sailing mostly on the American West Coast. The *Southward* was sold to Britain's Airtours for fly-cruising as the *Seawing* in 1995; the *Sun Princess* became the *Starship Majestic* for Premier Cruises Lines in 1989 and then the *Southern Cross* for CTC Lines in 1995.   *P&O Group*

Built originally at Genoa's Ansaldo shipyard, Swedish American Line's *Gripsholm* was delivered in the spring of 1957 and quickly rated as one of the most handsome new liners afloat. She divided her time between Atlantic crossings and mostly long, luxurious cruises until sold, in 1975, to Greece's Karageorgis Cruises. Renamed *Navarino*, she was sold again in 1981, to the Commodore Cruise Lines, who planned to use her in Miami-Caribbean service. But just before the sale was finalized, on November 26th, she was in a floating dock at Skaramanga, Greece which took on a 35-degree list. Badly flooded, the *Navarino* was considered a complete loss. But several months later, in May, she was righted, repaired and offered for resale. In 1983, she was sold to Italian interests known as Multiship Italia, who renamed her *Samantha,* the only liner ever to be registered in Rome. But there were financial problems and so the ship spent all of her time in lay-up. She was finally sold to Regency Cruises in October 1984 and was further refitted as their *Regent Sea*. She has since sailed in their Caribbean, Alaskan and South American cruise services. In 1996 she is due to sail again as the *Gripsholm* under charter to a German tour group.   *Steffen Weirauch*

In June 1989, when she arrived in Genoa, at least two local newspapers called her 'the death ship'. She was the onetime Swedish liner *Stockholm*, built in 1948, which rammed and sank the pride of the Italian fleet, the *Andrea Doria*, on a foggy night off New England in July 1956. But after an extended career as an East German trade union cruiseship, the *Volkerfreundschaft*, and then further work as a hotelship for Asian refugees, she had reached the Italian port to be rebuilt as a contemporary cruiseship. Starlauro was then running the *Achille Lauro* and a chartered ship, the *Amalfi*, a 6,600-tonner that had been Bergen Line's *Leda* in earlier days. They wanted additional cruise tonnage and so looked to the 525-foot long ex-*Stockholm*. First thought to be called *Sorrento*, the name *Positano* was

the favored choice by the summer of 1989. Later, *Surriento* was said to be considered. But the project was only half-complete by 1993. There had been long delays, reconstruction problems and errors, and difficulties with financing. Starlauro had long since abandoned any interest and instead the ship was renamed *Italia Prima*. Her actual owners are the Nina Cruise Lines, Nina coming from New Italian Navigation Ability. After sea trials, which were run in September 1994, she entered Mediterranean cruise service, mostly from Civitavecchia. It is an extraordinary re-emergence of what is basically a 46-year-old passenger ship. The two views show her in drydock at Genoa on August 27th 1994.

Maurizio Eliseo

Chapter Eleven
Italian Newbuildings

After the great heyday of Italian passenger ship construction in the 1950s and '60s, there seemed to be a long gap. But by the late 1980s, the reorganized and greatly modernized Fincantieri shipyards (officially Fincantieri Navali Italiani SpA) landed some impressive orders. Until then the Finns, the French and West Germans had dominated the market for cruiseships. These new Italian orders were in fact prompted by enthusiastic support from the Italian Government, which extended liberal construction subsidies (often as much as 50%) to shipowners. Comparatively, the Finns and the West Germans did not give subsidies and the French offered only as much as 25%. Politicians in Rome saw these subsidies as a way of providing much-needed work for Italian shipbuilders, their support firms and for Italian seamen. It also usually meant Italian registry for these new ships. In rather quick time, as many as eight large liners, each of them over 50,000 tons, resulted from these arrangements. P&O's *Crown Princess* was the first in this new group.

Above and below: The two new ships, the *Crown Princess* (shown under construction) and her sister, the *Regal Princess*, were the largest liners yet built in Italy (at a combined cost of over $400 million). At over 70,000 tons each, they surpassed the record held by the 51,000-ton *Rex*, completed in 1932.

P&O Group

Above: The 1,990-passenger *Crown Princess* was the first to be completed and was assigned to P&O's Los Angeles-based Princess Cruises subsidiary. She was floated out of her building slip at Monfalcone on May 25th 1989 and then delivered thirteen months later to a specially created P&O-Italian owner, Astramar SpA of Palermo. Ironically, the largest P&O passenger ship yet built was under the Italian flag (it has since been changed to Liberia).

Below: After a series of Mediterranean 'shakedown' cruises (the *Crown Princess* is shown passing Istanbul), the 804-foot liner crossed to New York in September 1990 for her formal christening and introduction.   *Both, Princess Cruises*

Left: At New York, during an extensive and expensive series of gala introductions (including fireworks along the Hudson River), the 22-knot liner was formally christened by legendary Italian film star Sophia Loren. For photographic purposes that included a better perspective of the famed Lower Manhattan skyline as a backdrop, the *Crown Princess* was berthed at an otherwise unused cargo terminal in Brooklyn Heights (a container dock in Bayonne, New Jersey had been the previous choice). Later, some cast members of television's 'Love Boat' joined the Royal Family of Monaco for a special charity-sponsored 'cruise to nowhere'.

Below: Decorative splendor in the '90s: The three-deck high atrium of the *Crown Princess* is highlighted by a grand staircase, a granite and bronze water sculpture as well as a shopping galleria, a 24-hour reception desk, a wine bar and a patisserie. *Both, Princess Cruises*

Begun by the Norwegian *Sea Goddess* twins of 1983-84, the idea of small, yacht-like, luxury cruiseships began to arouse interest in other shipowners as well. The Italian Government was amongst them and, in buoyant enthusiasm, they underwrote the construction of no less than eight luxury ships. There were in fact two sets of 100-passenger, 4,500-ton sisters. The *Renaissance Two*, shown outbound from Copenhagen on June 16th 1990, was part of the first series: *Renaissance One*, *Renaissance Two*, *Renaissance Three* and *Renaissance Four*. Heavily subsidized, these ships were intended to give work to two small Italian shipyards and were built in a two-year period between 1989 and 1991.

Ove Nielsen

The second series was slightly different in design and consisted of the *Renaissance Five* (shown berthed at Valletta with the German cruiseship *Arkona* arriving in the background in April 1993), *Renaissance Six*, *Renaissance Seven* and *Renaissance Eight*. The ships were chartered to Norway's Fearnley & Eger, but when that firm went bankrupt, in 1991, these 'yachts' fell on hard times as well. Two were arrested for debt. The Italian bank that held their mortgage ran them, but with diffculties. Two of them were later placed on charter to the Germans - the *Renaissance Five* became the *Hanseatic Renaissance* while the *Renaissance Eight* became the *Regina Renaissance*. Slumps in worldwide cruising also caused periodic lay-ups. The *Renaissance One* has since been sold to Singapore buyers for use as a casino ship. By 1991-92, the ships were running mostly 7-day cruises; the Caribbean, Scandinavia, the Mediterranean and East Africa. Their owners have become Renaissance Cruises, a partnership betwen Italy's Cameli Group, an industrial combine, and Luxury Liners Limited, a subsidiary of Florida-based Certified Tours.

Michael Cassar

Costa Cruises selected the Fincantieri yards for their two 53,000-tonners which are listed in the chapter on Costa. But it was especially noteworthy when Fincantieri also received an order for three (and later a fourth) 55,000-ton ships from Miami's Carnival Cruise Group, the parent of the legendary Holland America Line. The initial order was worth $750 million and has since surpassed $1 billion. These 1,266-passenger ships, initially dubbed the 'S class' - the *Statendam*, the *Stellendam* and the *Schiedam* - were the largest Holland America liners yet built, as well as being amongst the most beautiful ships of recent years. Shortly after her maiden voyage in January 1993, one US cruise editor dubbed the *Statendam* as 'one of the three or four best decorated ships afloat today'. The ship is shown at Lisbon with Starlauro's *Monterey* just ahead of her.

Luis Miguel Correia

These new Holland America liners
follow the Company's highly
successful, French-built pair of
Nieuw Amsterdam and *Noordam* of
1983-84, which blended high-
standard contemporary decor with
extensive collections of themed
artwork and antiques. Blended with
such features as a Murano glass
ceiling in the *Statendam*'s Rotterdam
Dining Room, the ship has a
$2million collection of art treasures
depicting early Dutch history and
its great age of exploration. Even the
liner's Lido Pool has a special
sculpture of mounted dolphins.

Holland America Line

Above: The name *Stellendam* soon gave way to *Maasdam* for the second in this Italian-built series. She is shown arriving in New York from Italy in November 1993. *Below:* The third ship was completed at Fincantieri as the *Ryndam* in the summer of 1994. The fourth ship of the class, due in 1996, will be the *Veendam.* In addition, Holland America's parent, the Carnival Cruise Group, have at least one 100,000-ton ship on order with Fincantieri for their own account. A 62,000-tonner, dubbed the '*Fastdam*' because of her high, 25-knot speed, has also been ordered from Fincantieri for Holland America. *Both, Holland America Line*

In the early 1990s, the newest entry in the expanding luxury cruise trade was Silversea Cruises, owned by the V Group of Monte Carlo (the former owners of the Sitmar passenger fleet) and the Lefevre family of Rome. When seeking builders, Silversea found the Italians most accommodating with their generous subsidies toward each of two $125 million vessels. The contracts went to the Societa Esercizio Cantieri of Viareggio. However, they allotted the building contracts to two other firms and so the hulls were launched at Donada (south of Venice) by the Visentini shipyard and then towed to Genoa and fitted out by the Mariotti company. At 15,000 tons, the 314-passenger *Silver Cloud* was delivered in April 1994, followed by a maiden cruise from Civitavecchia. The *Silver Wind* followed early in 1995. Both ships offer worldwide itineraries. *Luis Miguel Correia*

In the summer of 1993, cruise lines such as Carnival, Crystal and Celebrity announced new tonnage. And so, as if not to be left out, the California-based, but P&O-owned, Princess Cruises, one of the three largest firms in North American cruising, revealed plans for the 'super Love Boat'. The order for this mega-liner, a 77,000-tonner named *Sun Princess* (and later followed by sister-ship, the *Dawn Princess*), went to Fincantieri, which had then recently built the 70,000-ton sisters *Crown Princess* and *Regal Princess*. The 1,950-passenger *Sun Princess* had her maiden voyage, on the 7-day Port Everglades-Caribbean run, in December 1995. Her sister follows in the spring of 1997. *Princess Cruises*

Left: Along with a series of 70,000-ton cruiseships from Finland, Miami's Carnival Cruise Lines turned to the Italians as well in 1993. They ordered at least one 95,000-ton super-cruiseship that would carry up to 3,300 passengers in the Miami-Caribbean trade. However, soon after the announcement from Princess that they would build a 100,000-tonner in Italy, Carnival reassessed its specifications and found its new ship would be 'at least 100,000 tons'. At this stage, she was dubbed the 'Big Mama', but at the time of writing her official name seems likely to be *Carnival Destiny*.
Carnival Cruise Lines

Below: In peaked optimism for the American cruise trades and in the wake of their twin 77,000-tonners, Princess Cruises placed an order with Fincantieri for one 100,000-ton cruiseship, the *Grand Princess*.Due out in the fall of 1997, her design will include such notable features as a virtual reality theatre, three main show-rooms, three dining rooms, 750 cabins with verandas, five pools and a unique nightclub positioned 15 decks above the sea and accessible only by a suspended glass-enclosed walkway. The 2,600-passenger ship is aimed at the Port Everglades-Caribbean 7-day cruise trade.
Princess Cruises

Epilogue

Normally, by late November the New York City Passenger Ship Terminal is darkened and empty. It is almost completely closed in the winter. But on a night in November 1993, the Terminal lights were ablaze. A liner was in port and not only was she unique in remaining overnight, but it was her maiden voyage. Under a deep, charcoal-colored sky, Holland America Line's 55,451-ton *Maasdam* sparkled amidst her own lights - a floodlit funnel, rows of twinkling windows and portholes, a long strand of fairy lights and even her own name spelled out in marquee-style bulbs. Endless reflections shimmered off the Hudson River water and bounced off her pristine, dark blue hull.

Invited guests - cruise editors and publishers, travel writers, other journalists, friends and selected, top-selling travel agents - began arriving in the late afternoon. They went aboard to toast the $250 million ship and to spend the night, a sort of dockside "cruise to nowhere." Soon, sounds filled the ship - a string quartet, conversations in lounges and the entrance lobby and along seemingly endless corridors, and inevitably the clinking of crystal glasses filled with champagne. The *Maasdam* herself was radiant. Every tabletop shimmered, every piece of art polished, every carpet freshened. Guests began to move about - there was a presentation of welcoming gifts, the Chairman's cocktail party, travelogues showing in the theatre, a floor show with a Broadway star and later a gala dinner in the two-deck high dining room.

The 720-foot long, 1,266-passenger *Maasdam* had arrived that same morning from her Italian birthplace at the Fincantieri yard at Monfalcone. The crossing took fifteen days ("a bouncy trip," noted one Indonesian waiter) and included a short call at Boston. Then, after New York, the ship visited other US East Coast ports as part of her "inaugural show-off" before taking up station at Port Everglades. That first call included the ship's official baptism, a christening and naming ceremony presided over by Hollywood film star June Allyson. The ship then spent the winter running Caribbean and trans-Panama Canal cruises before going onto Holland America's Vancouver-Alaska run for the summer.

It took a little over two years for Fincantieri to complete the *Maasdam*. She is the second in a set of four - the *Statendam* arrived ten months before, in January; the *Ryndam* followed in another ten months, in September 1994; the *Veendam*, in May 1996. They are the largest, most expensive and perhaps the most luxuriously comfortable Holland America liners ever built. The Seattle-based company might have gone to the French (who built the earlier *Nieuw Amsterdam* and *Noordam* of 1983-84), the Germans or the Finns, but it was the Italians who landed yet another prestigious contract. The Dutch were joining the likes of Princess, Costa, Renaissance, Silversea and Carnival itself (the parent of Holland America) in using Italian shipyards. This new armada follows worthily in the historic wake of so many of the passenger ships listed in these pages - the *Saturnia*, the *Giulio Cesare*, the *Michelangelo*, the *Galileo Galilei* and the *Eugenio C.*

Bibliography

Bonsor, N.R.P. *North Atlantic Seaway.* Prescot, Lancashire: T. Stephenson & Sons Ltd, 1955.

Bonsor, N.R.P. *South Atlantic Seaway.* Jersey, Channel Islands: Brookside Publications, 1983.

Braynard, Frank O. & Miller, William H. *Fifty Famous Liners, Vols 1-3.*
Cambridge: Patrick Stephens Ltd, 1982-1986.

Cooke, Anthony. *Emigrant Ships.* London: Carmania Press, 1992.

Crowdy, Michael (editor). *Marine News (1964-1994).* Kendal, Cumbria: World Ship Society.

Devol, George (editor). *Ocean & Cruise News (1980-1994).* Stamford, Connecticut: World Ocean & Cruise Society.

Dunn, Laurence. *Passenger Liners.* Southampton: Adlard Coles Ltd, 1961.

Dunn, Laurence. *Passenger Liners (revised edition).* Southampton: Adlard Coles Ltd, 1965.

Eisele, Peter & Rau, William (editors). *Steamboat Bill (1966-1994).* New York: Steamship Historical Society of America Inc.

Kludas, Arnold. *Great Passenger Ships of the World, Vols 1-5.* Cambridge: Patrick Stephens Ltd, 1972-1976.

Kludas, Arnold. *Great Passenger Ships of the World, Vol 6.* Cambridge: Patrick Stephens Ltd, 1986.

Kludas, Arnold. *Great Passenger Ships of the World Today.* Sparkford: Patrick Stephens Ltd, 1992.

Miller, William H. *The Cruiseships.* London: Conway Maritime Press Ltd, 1988.

Miller, William H. *The Last Atlantic Liners.* London: Conway Maritime Press Ltd, 1985.

Miller, William H. *The Last Blue Water Liners.* London: Conway Maritime Press Ltd, 1986.

Miller, William H. *Transatlantic Liners 1945-1980.* Newton Abbot, Devon: David & Charles Ltd, 1981.

Plowman, Peter. *Emigrant Ships To Luxury Liners.* Kensington, Australia: New South Wales University Press, 1992.

Sawyer, L.A. & Mitchell, W.H. *From America to United States, Vols 1-4.* Kendal, Cumbria: World Ship Society, 1979-1986.

Shopland, Robert (editor). *Ships Monthly (1982-1994).* Burton-on-Trent: Waterway Productions Ltd.

Towline. (1950-1994). New York: Moran Towing & Transportation Co.

Specifications of the Ships

Achille Lauro
Built by De Schelde Shipyards, Flushing, Netherlands, 1939-47. 23,629 gross tons; 631 feet long; 82 feet wide. Sulzer diesels, twin screw. Service speed 22 knots. Approximately 1,652 passengers (152 first class, approximately 1,500 tourist class).

Africa
Built by Cantieri Riuniti dell 'Adriatico, Monfalcone, Italy, 1952. 11,434 gross tons; 523 feet long; 68 feet wide. Fiat diesels, twin screw. Service speed 19 ½ knots. 446 passengers (148 first class, 298 tourist class).

Amercian Adventure (see *Costa Riviera*)

Amerigo Vespucci
Built Ansaldo SpA, Genoa, Italy, 1942-48. 9,774 gross tons; 485 feet long; 62 feet wide. Fiat diesel, single screw. Service speed 15 knots. 526 passengers (90 cabin class, 436 third class).

Andrea C.
Built by Todd-California Shipbuilding Corporation, Richmond, California, 1942. 8,604 gross tons; 467 feet long; 57 feet wide. Fiat diesel, single screw. Service speed 16 knots. 482 passengers (variable from 122 first class and 354 tourist class or 234 first class and 248 tourist class).

Andrea Doria
Built by Ansaldo SpA, Genoa, Italy, 1953. 29,083 gross tons; 700 feet long; 90 feet wide. Steam turbines, twin screw. Service speed 23 knots. 1,304 passengers (281 first class, 320 cabin class, 703 tourist class).

Andrea Gritti
Built by Cantieri Riuniti dell 'Adriatico, Monfalcone, Italy, 1943. 8,072 gross tons; 470 feet long; 60 feet wide. Diesel, single screw. Service speed 14 ½ knots. 550 third class passengers.

Angelina Lauro
Built by Netherlands Shipbuilding Company, Amsterdam, Netherlands, 1939. 24,377 gross tons; 672 feet long; 83 feet wide. Sulzer diesels, triple screw. Service speed 21 ½ knots. 1,616 passengers (189 first class, 1,427 tourist class).

Anna C.
Built by Lithgows Ltd, Glasgow, Scotland, 1929. 12,030 gross tons; 524 feet long; 65 feet wide. Fiat diesels, twin screw. Service speed 20 knots. 1,066 passengers (202 first class, 864 tourist class).

Antonio Usodimare
Built 1942-49 - otherwise see *Amerigo Vespucci*.

Argentina
Built by Cammell Laird & Company Limited, Birkenhead, England, 1913. 11,015 gross tons; 530 feet long; 61 feet wide. Steam turbines, twin screw. Service speed 15 knots. 1,001 passengers (32 first class, 969 tourist class).

Ascania
Built by Ateliers et Chantiers de la Loire, St Nazaire, France, 1926. 9,536 gross tons; 490 feet long; 60 feet wide. Steam turbines, twin screw. Service speed 16 knots. 1,247 passengers (87 first class, 1,160 tourist class).

Asia
Built by Cantieri Riuniti dell 'Adriatico, Monfalcone, Italy, 1953. 11, 693 gross tons; 522 feet long; 68 feet wide. Fiat diesels, twin screw. Service speed 19 ½ knots. 431 passengers (290 first class, 141 tourist class).

Atlantic - 1927
Built by William Cramp & Sons Ship & Engine Building Company, Philadelphia, Pennsylvania, 1927. 20,553 gross tons; 582 feet long; 83 feet wide. Steam turbines, twin screw. Service speed 21 knots. 1,179 passengers (132 first class, 116 cabin class, 931 tourist class).

Atlantic - 1981
Built by CNIM Shipyards, La Seyne, France, 1981. 30,262 gross tons; 672 feet long; 90 feet wide. Fiat diesels, twin screw. Service speed 23 knots. 1,179 cruise passengers.

Augustus
Built by Cantieri Riuniti dell 'Adriatico, Trieste, Italy, 1952. 27,090 gross tons; 680 feet long; 87 feet wide. Fiat diesels, twin screw. Service speed 21 knots. 1,174 passengers (180 first class, 280 cabin class, 714 tourist class).

Aurelia
Built by Blohm & Voss, Hamburg, Germany, 1939. 10,480 gross tons; 487 feet long; 60 feet wide. Diesel-electric, single screw. Service speed 17 knots. 1,124 tourist class passengers.

Ausonia
Built by Cantieri Riuniti dell 'Adriatico, Monfalcone, Italy, 1957. 11,879 gross tons; 522 feet long; 70 feet wide. Steam turbines, twin screw. Service speed 20 knots. 529 passengers (181 first class, 118 second class, 230 third class).

Australia
Built by Cantieri Riuniti dell 'Adriatico, Trieste, Italy, 1951. 13,140 gross tons; 528 feet long; 69 feet wide. Sulzer diesels, twin screw. Service speed 18 knots. 672 passengers (136 first class, 304 tourist class, 232 third class).

Bernina
Built by Ansaldo SpA, Leghorn, Italy, 1959. 4,400 gross tons; 385 feet long; 54 feet wide. Fiat diesels, twin screw. Service speed 16 knots. 81 first class passengers.

Bianca C.
Built by Constructions Navales, La Ciotat, France, 1939-49. 18,427 gross tons; 594 feet long; 75 feet wide. Sulzer diesels, triple screw. Service speed 21 knots. 1,232 passengers (202 first class, 1,030 tourist class).

Brasil
Built by Alexander Stephen & Sons Limited, Glasgow, Scotland, 1905. 10,043 gross tons; 538 feet long; 60 feet wide. Steam turbines, triple screw. Service speed 18 knots. 942 passengers (96 first class, 846 tourist class).

Brennero - See *Bernina*
Caribia - See *Vulcania*
Caribia 2 - See *Sydney*

Carnival Destiny
Building by Fincantieri Shipyards, Monfalcone, Italy, 1997. 105,000 gross tons. Diesels, twin screw. Service speed 21 knots. 3,300 maximum cruise passengers.

Carla C./Carla Costa
Built by Ateliers et Chantiers de France, Dunkirk, France, 1952. 19,975 gross tons; 600 feet long; 80 feet wide. Diesels, twin screw. Service speed 21 knots. 754 cruise passengers.

Castel Bianco
Built by Bethlehem-Fairfield Shipyard, Baltimore, Maryland, USA, 1945. 7,604 gross tons; 455 feet long; 62 feet wide. Steam turbines, single screw. Service speed 16 knots. 800 third class pasengers.

Castel Felice
Built by Alexander Stephen & Sons Limited, Glasgow, Scotland, 1930. 12,478 gross tons; 493 feet long; 64 feet wide. Steam turbines, twin screw. Service speed 17 knots. 1,405 tourist class passengers.

Castel Verde
Built by California Shipbuilding Corporation, Los Angeles, California, USA, 1945. 7,607 gross tons; 455 feet long; 62 feet wide. Steam turbines, single screw. Service speed 16 knots. 800 third class passengers.

Columbus C.
Built by De Schelde Shipyards, Flushing, Netherlands, 1953. 21,141 gross tons; 600 feet long; 77 feet wide. B&W diesels, twin screw. Service speed 19 knots. 802 cruise passengers.

Conte Biancamano
Built by William Beardmore & Company, Glasgow, Scotland, 1925. 23,842 gross tons; 665 feet long; 76 feet wide. Steam turbines, twin screw. Service speed 18 knots. 1,578 passengers (215 first class, 333 cabin class, 1,030 tourist class).

Conte Grande
Built by Stabilimento Tecnico, Trieste, Italy, 1928. 23,562 gross tons; 667 feet long; 78 feet wide. Steam turbines, twin screw. Service speed 18 knots. 1,379 passengers (261 first class, 338 cabin class, 780 tourist class).

Costa Allegra
Built by Wartsila Shipyards, Abo, Finland, 1969. 25,500 gross tons; 572 feet long; 83 feet wide. Pielstick diesels, twin screw. Service speed 19 knots. 1,066 maximum cruise passengers.

Costa Classica
Built by Fincantieri Shipyards, Venice, Italy, 1991. 53,700 gross tons; 723 feet long; 98 feet wide. Diesels, twin screw. Service speed 20 knots. 1,300 maximum cruise passengers.

Costa Marina
Built by Wartsila Shipyards, Abo, Finland, 1969. 25,441 gross tons; 572 feet long; 84 feet wide. Pielstick diesels, twin screw. Service speed 19 knots. 1,025 maximum cruise passengers.

Costa Riviera
Built by Cantieri dell 'Adriatico, Monfalcone, Italy, 1963. 31,500 gross tons; 702 feet long; 94 feet wide. Steam turbines, twin screw. Service speed 24 knots. 984 cruise passengers.

Costa Romantica
1993 - otherwise see *Costa Classica*

Costa Victoria
Built at Bremer Vulkan Shipyard, Bremen, Germany, 1996. 73,000 gross tons. Diesels, twin screw. Service speed 21 knots. 1,900 maximum cruise passengers.

Cristoforo Colombo
Built by Ansaldo SpA, Genoa, Italy, 1954. 29,191 gross tons; 700 feet long; 90 feet wide. Steam turbines, twin screw. Service speed 23 knots. 1,246 passengers (301 first class, 242 cabin class, 703 tourist class).

Crown Princess
Built by Fincantieri Shipyards, Monfalcone, Italy, 1990. 69,845 gross tons; 804 feet long; 105 fet wide. M.A.N.-B&W diesels, twin screw. Service speed 19 ½ knots. 1,990 maximum cruise passengers.

Danae
Built by Harland & Wolff Limited, Belfast, Northern Ireland, 1955. 16,310 gross tons; 533 feet long; 70 feet wide. Burmeister & Wain diesels, twin screw. Service speed 17 knots. Approximately 500 cruise passengers.

Daphne
Built by Swan, Hunter & Wigham Richardson Limited, Newcastle, England, 1955. Doxford diesels. Otherwise see *Danae*.

Dawn Princess
1997 - otherwise see *Sun Princess*.

Donizetti
Built by Cantieri Riuniti dell 'Adriatico, Trieste, Italy, 1951. 13,226 gross tons; 528 feet long; 69 feet wide. Sulzer diesels, twin screw. Service speed 17 ½ knots. 600 passengers (160 first class, 440 tourist class).

Doric
Built by Chantiers de l'Atlantique, St Nazaire, France, 1964. 25,320 gross tons; 629 feet long; 82 feet wide. Steam turbines, twin screw. Service speed 20 knots. 945 cruise passengers.

Enotria
Built by Ansaldo SpA, Leghorn, Italy, 1951. 5,173 gross tons; 383 feet long; 54 feet wide. Fiat diesels, twin screw. Service speed 16 knots. 268 passengers (120 first class, 148 tourist class).

Enrico C./Enrico Costa
Built by Swan, Hunter & Wigham Richardson Limited, Newcastle, England, 1951. 13,607 gross tons; 580 feet long; 73 feet wide. Steam turbines, twin screw. Service speed 18 knots. 1,198 passengers (218 first class, 980 tourist class).

Esperia
Built by Cantieri Riuniti dell 'Adriatico, Monfalcone, Italy, 1949. 9,314 gross tons; 488 feet long; 63 feet wide. Sulzer diesels, twin screw. Service speed 19 ½ knots. 504 passengers (159 first class, 81 second class, 264 third class).

Eugenio C./Eugenio Costa
Built by Cantieri Riuniti dell 'Adriatico, Monfalcone, Italy, 1966. 30,567 gross tons; 712 feet ong; 96 feet wide. Steam turbines, twin screw. Service speed 27 knots. 1,636 passengers (178 first class, 356 cabin class, 1,102 tourist class).

Europa - 1923
Built by Sir W.G. Armstrong-Whitworth & Company Limited, Newcastle, England, 1923. 15,043 gross tons; 573 feet long; 72 feet wide. Steam turbines, twin screw. Service speed 17 knots. 617 one-class passengers.

Europa - 1952
Built by Ansaldo SpA, Genoa, Italy, 1952. 11,440 gross tons; 522 feet long; 68 feet wide. Fiat diesels, twin screw. Service speed 19 ½ knots. 446 passengers (148 first class, 298 tourist class).

Fairsea - 1941
Built by Sun Shipbuilding & Dry Dock Company, Chester, Pennsylvania, USA, 1941. 13,432 gross tons; 492 feet long; 69 feet wide. Doxford diesel, single screw. Service speed 16 knots. 1,460 tourist class passengers.

Fairsea - 1956
Built by John Brown & Company Limited, Clydebank, Scotland, 1956. 21,916 gross tons; 608 feet long; 80 feet wide. Steam turbines, twin screw. Service speed 19 ½ knots. 910 cruise passengers.

Fairsky - 1941
Built by Western Pipe & Steel Company, San Francisco, California, USA, 1941. 12,464 gross tons; 502 feet long; 69 feet wide. Steam turbines, twin screw. Service speed 18 knots. 1,461 tourist class passengers.

Fairsky - 1961
Built by Swan, Hunter & Wigham Richardson Limited, Newcastle, England, 1961. 19,393 gross tons; 625 feet long; 78 feet wide. Steam turbines, twin screw. Service speed 20 knots. 1,200 maximum passengers.

Fairsky - 1984
Built by CNIM Shipyards, La Seyne, France, 1984. 46,314 gross tons; 790 feet long; 90 feet wide. Steam turbines, twin screw. Service speed 19 knots. 1,212 cruise passengers.

Fairstar
Built by Fairfield Shipbuilding & Engineering Company, Glasgow, Scotland, 1957. 23,764 gross tons; 609 feet long; 78 feet wide. Steam turbines, twin screw. Service speed 20 knots. 1,910 tourist class passengers.

Fairwind - See Fairsea

Federico C.
Built by Ansaldo SpA, Genoa, Italy, 1958. 20,416 gross tons; 606 feet long; 79 feet wide. Steam turbines, twin screw. Service speed 21 knots. 1,279 passengers (243 first class, 300 cabin class, 736 tourist class).

Flaminia
Built by Merchant Shipbuilding Corporation, Chester, Pennsylvania, USA, 1922. 8,776 gross tons; 462 feet long; 60 feet wide. Sulzer diesels, twin screw. Service speed 14 ½ knots. 1,024 tourist class passengers.

Flavia
Built by John Brown & Company Limited, Clydebank, Scotland, 1947. 15,465 gross tons; 556 feet long; 70 feet wide. Steam turbines, twin screw. Service speed 18 knots. 1,220 tourist class passengers.

Florentia
Built by William Denny & Brothers Limited, Dumbarton, Scotland, 1914. 7,821 gross tons; 484 feet long; 58 feet wide. Steam triple expansion, single screw. Service speed 13 knots. 1,000 passengers.

Franca C.
Built by Newport News Shipbuilding & Dry Dock Company, Newport News, Virginia, USA, 1914. 6,822 gross tons; 428 feet long; 55 feet wide. Fiat diesel, single screw. Service speed 15 knots. 367 cruise passengers.

Francesco Morosini
Built by Cantieri Riuniti dell 'Adriatico, Monfalcone, Italy, 1948. 8,678 gross tons; 470 feet long; 60 feet wide. Diesel, single screw. Service speed 14 ½ knots. 550 third class passengers.

Fulvia
Built by Netherlands Shipbuilding Company, Amsterdam, Netherlands, 1949. 16,844 gross tons; 577 feet long; 72 feet wide. Stork diesels, twin screw. Service speed 20 knots. 646 maximum cruise passengers.

Galileo Galilei
Built by Cantieri Riuniti dell 'Adriatico, Monfalcone, Italy, 1963. 27,907 gross tons; 702 feet long; 94 feet wide. Steam turbines, twin screw. Service speed 24 knots. 1,750 passengers (156 first class, 1,594 tourist class).

Genova - See *Flaminia*

Giulio Cesare
Built by Cantieri Riuniti dell 'Adriatico, Monfalcone, Italy, 1951. 27,078 gross tons; 681 feet long; 87 feet wide. Fiat diesels, twin screw. Service speed 21 knots. 1,183 passengers (181 first class, 288 cabin class, 714 tourist class).

Grand Princess
Building by Fincantieri Shipyards, Monfalcone, Italy, 1997. Approximately 100,000 gross tons. Diesels, twin screw. Service speed approximately 21 knots. 3,500 maximum cruise passengers.

Guglielmo Marconi
27,905 gross tons - otherwise see *Galileo Galilei*.

Homeland - See *Brasil*

Homeric - 1931
Built by Bethlehem Steel Company, Quincy, Massachusetts, 1931. 24,907 gross tons; 638 feet long; 79 feet wide. Steam turbines, twin screw. Service speed 20 knots. 1,243 passengers (147 first class, 1,096 tourist class).

Homeric - 1986
Built by Joseph L. Meyer Shipyards, Papenburg, Germany, 1986. 42,092 gross tons; 668 feet long; 96 feet wide. M.A.N.-B&W diesels, twin screw. Service speed 22 knots. 1,085 cruise passengers.

Illiria
Built by Cantieri Navale Pellegrino, Naples, Italy, 1962. 3,763 gross tons; 333 feet long; 48 feet wide. Fiat diesels, twin screw. Service speed 17 knots. 180 cruise passengers.

Irpinia
Built by Swan, Hunter & Wigham Richardson Limited, Newcastle, England, 1929. 13,204 gross tons; 537 feet long; 67 feet wide. Fiat diesels, twin screw. Service speed 16 knots. 1,181 passengers (209 first class, 972 tourist class).

Italia - 1928
Built by Blohm & Voss, Hamburg, Germany, 1928. 21,532 gross tons; 609 feet long; 78 feet wide. B&W diesels, twin screw. Service speed 17 knots. 1,319 passengers (213 first class, 1,106 tourist class).

Italia - 1967
Built by Cantieri Navali Feszegi Shipyards, Trieste, Italy, 1967. 12,219 gross tons; 490 feet long; 68 feet wide. Sulzer diesels, twin screw. Service speed 20 knots. 476 cruise passengers.

Italia Prima
Built by Gotaverken, Gothenburg, Sweden, 1948. 15,200 gross tons; 525 feet long; 69 feet wide. Wartsila diesels, twin screw. Service speed 19 knots. 580 cruise passengers.

Leonardo Da Vinci
Built by Ansaldo SpA, Genoa, Italy, 1960. 33,340 gross tons; 761 feet long; 92 feet wide. Steam turbines, twin screw. Service speed 23 knots. 1,326 passengers (413 first class, 342 cabin class, 571 tourist class).

Liguria
Built by Reiherstieg Shipyard, Hamburg, Germany, 1914. 7,474 gross tons; 426 feet long; 55 feet wide. Steam quadruple expansion engines, twin screw. Service speed 14 knots. 925 third class passengers.

Lucania
Built by Cammell Laird & Company Limited, Birkenhead, England, 1930. 6,723 gross tons; 400 feet long; 57 feet wide. Steam turbines, twin screw. Service speed 20 knots. 970 passengers (170 first class, 800 third class).

Luciano Manara
Built by Ansaldo SpA, Genoa, Italy, 1941. 8,333 gross tons; 472 feet long; 62 feet wide. Diesel, single screw. Service speed 15 knots. 700 third class passengers.

Lugano
Built by R. & W. Hawthorn Leslie, Newcastle, England, 1898. 6,942 gross tons; 421 feet long; 54 feet wide. Steam triple expansion engines, single screw. Service speed 11 knots. 1,000 third class passengers.

Maasdam
Built by Fincantieri Shipyards, Monfalcone, Italy, 1993. 55,400 gross tons; 720 feet long; 90 feet wide. Diesels, twin screw. Service speed 20 knots. 1,600 maximum cruise passengers.

Marco Polo
Built 1942-48 - otherwise see *Amerigo Vespucci*

Marengo - see *Urania II*

Melanesien
Built by De Schelde Shipyards, Flushing, Netherlands, 1925. 9,905 gross tons; 507 feet long; 60 feet wide. Sulzer diesels, twin screw. Service speed 15 knots. 180 passengers (100 first class, 80 third class).

Messapia - See *Enotria*

Michelangelo
Built by Ansaldo SpA, Genoa, Italy, 1965. 45,911 gross tons; 902 feet long; 102 feet wide. Steam turbines, twin screw. Service speed 26 ½ knots. 1,775 passengers (535 first class, 550 cabin class, 690 tourist class).

Monterey
Built by Bethlehem Steel Company, Sparrows Point, Maryland, USA, 1952. 14,799 gross tons; 563 feet long; 76 feet wide. Steam turbines, single screw. Service speed 20 knots. 600 cruise passengers.

Napoli
Built by Harland & Wolff Limited, Belfast, Northern Ireland, 1940. 8,082 gross tons; 451 feet long; 57 feet wide. Diesel, single screw. Service speed 14 knots. 650 passengers.

Nassau - See *Europa* - 1923

Neptunia - See *Australia*

Oceania - See *Australia*

Oceanic
Built by Cantieri Riuniti dell 'Adriatico, Monfalcone, Italy, 1965. 39,241 gross tons; 774 feet long; 96 feet wide. Steam turbines, twin screw. Service speed 26 ½ knots. 1,600 maximum passengers.

Olimpia
Built by St Johns River Shipbuilding Corporation, Jacksonville, Florida, 1943. 7,716 gross tons; 441 feet long; 57 feet wide. Steam triple expansion engines, single screw. Service speed 11 knots.

Pace
Built by Wiliam Cramp & Sons Ship & Engine Building Company, Philadelphia, Pennsylvania, USA, 1921. 4,013 gross tons; 325 feet long; 57 feet wide. Steam triple expansion engines, twin screw. Service speed 17 knots. 500 passengers.

Paolo Toscanelli
Built by Ansaldo SpA, Genoa, Italy, 1942-49. 9,004 gross tons; 485 feet long; 62 feet wide. Diesel, single screw. Service 15 ½ knots. Approximately 500 passengers in first and third class.

Raffaello
Built by Cantieri Riuniti dell 'Adriatico, Trieste, Italy, 1965. 45,933 gross tons; 902 feet long; 102 feet wide. Steam turbines, twin screw. Service speed 26 ½ knots. 1,775 passengers (535 first class, 550 cabin class, 690 tourist class).

Ravello
Built by Cantieri Navali Riuniti, Genoa, Italy, 1941. 8,806 gross tons; 458 feet long; 62 feet wide. Diesel, single screw. Service speed 16 knots. 480 passengers.

Regal Princess
1991 - otherwise see *Crown Princess*

Renaissance One - Renaissance Four
Built by Cantieri Navale Ferrari, Italy, 1989-90. 4,077 gross tons; 290 feet long; 50 feet wide. Diesels, twin screw. Service speed 15 knots. 100 cruise passengers.

Renaissance Five - Renaissance Eight
Built by Nuovi Cantieri Apuania SpA, Marina di Carrara, Italy, 1991. 4,280 gross tons; 297 feet long; 50 feet wide. Diesels, twin screw. Service speed 15 knots. 114 cruise passengers.

Repubblica Di Amalfi
Built by Fincantieri Shipyards, Castellamare di Stabia, Italy, 1989. 35,750 gross tons; 604 feet long; 99 feet wide. Sulzer diesels, single screw. Service speed 18 knots. 57 passengers.

Repubblica Di Genova
1988 - otherwise see *Repubblica Di Amalfi*

Repubblica Di Pisa
Built by Nouvi Cantieri Apuania SpA, Marina di Carrara, Italy, 1987. 39,294 gross tons; 594 feet long; 99 feet wide. Sulzer diesel, single screw. Service speed 18 knots. 54 passengers.

Repubblica Di Venezia
Built by Fincantieri Shipyards, Venice, Italy, 1987. Otherwise see *Repubblica Di Pisa*.

Rhapsody
Built by Burmeister & Wain Shipyards, Copenhagen, Denmark; completed by Industrie Navali Mechaniche Affine Shipyard, La Spezia, Italy, 1977. 17,496 gross tons; 536 feet long; 74 feet wide. B&W diesels, twin screw. Service speed 20 ½ knots. 750 cruise passengers.

Rio De La Plata
Built by Ansaldo SpA, Genoa, Italy, 1950. 11,317 gross tons; 550 feet long; 66 feet wide. Fiat diesels, twin screws. Service speed 18 knots. 116 first class passengers.

Rio Jachal - See *Rio De La Plata*

Rio Tunuyan - See *Rio De La Plata*

Riviera Prima
Built by Ateliers et Chantiers de la Loire, St Nazaire, France, 1950. 12,812 gross tons; 537 feet long; 64 feet wide. Sulzer diesels, twin screw. Service speed 16 knots. 600 cruise passengers.

Roma 1914 - See *Franca C.*

Roma - 1946
Built by Seattle-Tacoma Shipbuilding Corporation, Tacoma, Washington, USA, 1946. 14,687 gross tons; 492 feet long; 69 feet wide. Steam turbines, single screw. Service speed 17 knots. 1,113 passengers (119 first class, 994 tourist class).

Ryndam
1994 - otherwise see *Maasdam*

Rossini - See *Donizetti*

Samantha
Built Ansaldo SpA, Genoa, Italy, 1957. 23,191 gross tons; 631 feet long; 82 feet wide. Gotaverken diesels, twin screw. Service speed 19 knots. 800 cruise passengers.

San Giorgio
Built by Cantieri Riuniti dell 'Adriatico, Trieste, Italy, 1956. 4,755 gross tons; 367 feet long; 51 feet wide. Fiat diesels, twin screw. Service speed 17 knots. 203 passengers (92 first class, 45 second class, 66 tourist class).

San Marco - See *San Giorgio*

Saturnia
Built by Cantieri Navali Triestino, Monfalcone, Italy, 1927. 24,346 gross tons; 630 feet long; 80 feet wide. Sulzer diesels, twin screw. Service speed 19 knots. 1,479 passengers (255 first class, 270 cabin class, 954 tourist class).

Sebastiano Caboto - See *Paolo Toscanelli*

Sestriere
Built by Cantieri Navali Franco Tosi, Taranto, Italy, 1943. 8,652 gross tons; 476 feet long; 61 feet wide. Diesel, single screw. Service speed 14 knots. 550 third class passengers.

Silver Cloud
Built for Societa Esercizio Cantieri, Viareggio, Italy; completed by T. Mariotti Shipyard, Genoa, Italy, 1994. 16,800 gross tons;514 feet long; 70 feet wide. Diesels, twin screw. Service speed 20 ½ knots. 314 maximum cruise passengers.

Silver Wind - See *Silver Cloud*

Sises
Built by Canteri Navali di Taranto, Italy, 1948. 9,177 gross tons; 474 feet long; 62 feet wide. Diesel, single screw. Service speed 17 ½ knots. 550 third class passengers.

Southward
Built by Cantieri Navali del Tirreno e Riuniti SpA Shipyard, Genoa, Italy, 1971. 16,607 gross tons; 536 feet long; 75 feet wide. Fiat diesels, twin screw. Service speed 21 knots. 918 maximum cruise passengers.

Spirit of London
Built by Cantieri Navali del Tirreno e Riuniti SpA Shipyard, Genoa, Italy, 1972. 17,370 gross tons; 535 feet long; 75 feet wide. Fiat diesels, twin screw. Service speed 20 knots. 862 maximum cruise passengers.

Statendam
1992 - otherwise see *Maasdam*

Stelvio - See *Bernina*

Sun Princess
Built by Fincantieri Shipyards, Monfalcone, Italy, 1995. 77,000 gross tons; 855 feet long; 105 feet wide. Sulzer diesels, twin screw. Service speed 21 knots. 2,400 maximum cruise passengers.

Surriento
Built by Furness Shipbuilding Company, Haverton Hill, England, 1928. 11,500 gross tons; 498 feet long; 64 feet wide. Sulzer diesels, twin screw. Service speed 17 knots. 1,080 passengers (first and tourist class).

Sydney
Built by Western Pipe & Steel Company, San Francisco, California, USA, 1944 - otherwise see *Roma* - 1946.

Symphony - See *Enrico C.*

Toscana
Built by A.G. Weser Shipbuilders, Bremen, Germany, 1923. 9,584 gross tons; 480 feet long; 62 feet wide. Steam triple expansion engines, twin screw. Service speed 12 knots. 819 third class passengers.

Ugolino Vivaldi - See *Paolo Toscanelli*

Urania II
Built by Barclay, Curle Limited, Glasgow, Scotland, 1914. 6,715 gross tons; 440 feet long; 53 feet wide. Steam triple expansion engines, single screw. Service speed 12 ½ knots. 300 passengers.

Veendam - otherwise see *Maasdam*

Venezuela
Built by Cammell Laird & Company Limited, Birkenhead, England, 1924. 18,769 gross tons; 597 feet long; 71 feet wide. Steam turbines, twin screw. Service speed 18 knots. 1,480 passengers (180 first class, 500 cabin class, 800 tourist class).

Verdi - See *Donizetti*

Victoria - 1936
Built by Harland & Wolff Limited, Belfast, Northern Ireland, 1936. 14,917 gross tons; 573 feet long; 72 feet wide. Fiat diesels, twin screw. Service speed 18 knots. 600 cruise passengers.

Victoria - Lloyd Triestino
11,695 gross tons - otherwise see *Asia*.

Vulcania
Built by Cantieri Navali Triestino, Monfalcone, Italy, 1928. 24,496 gross tons; 631 feet long; 80 feet wide. Fiat diesels, twin screw. Service speed 19 knots. 1,452 passengers (232 first class, 262 cabin class, 958 tourist class).

Newbuilding, Walt Disney Cruise Lines
Building at Fincantieri Shipyards, Monfalcone, Italy, 1997-98. Approximately 85,000 ross tons. Diesels, twin screw. 2,400 maximum cruise passengers.

Newbuilding No. 2, Walt Disney Cruise Lines
1998 - otherwise see previous newbuilding.